SUPER-SILLY HERO SKITS FOR CHILDREN'S MINISTRY

by
Christopher P. N. Maselli

Carson-Dellosa Publishing Company, Inc.
Greensboro, North Carolina

It is the mission of Carson-Dellosa to create the highest-quality Scripture-based children's products that teach the Word of God, share His love and goodness, assist in faith development, and glorify His Son, Jesus Christ."

". . . teach me your ways so I may know you. . . ."
Exodus 33:13

For Van and Tena Walker for believing in heroes, both in the audience and on-stage.

CREDITS

Editor .... Kathie Szitas
Layout Design............ Clint Moore
Inside Illustrations ... Ray Lambert
Cover Design .... Peggy Jackson
Cover Illustration ..... Ray Lambert

Unless otherwise noted, Scripture is taken from the HOLY BIBLE, NEW INTERNATIONAL VERSION®. Copyright © 1973, 1978, 1984 by International Bible Society. Used by permission of Zondervan Bible Publishers.

Scripture quotations marked NLT are taken from the *Holy Bible*, New Living Translation, copyright 1996. Used by permission of Tyndale House Publishers, Inc., Wheaton, Illinois 60189. All rights reserved.

Scripture on the back cover is taken from THE MESSAGE. Copyright © 1993, 1994, 1995, 1996, 2000, 2001, 2002. Used by permission of NavPress Publishing Group.

ISBN 978-1-60022-442-3

TABLE OF CONTENTS

INFORMATION FOR MORTALS

WELCOME to *Super-Silly Hero Skits*—a collection of 12 hilarious five-minute skits that you can use with your children's church, Sunday school, or other ministry opportunities. Each skit requires only two adults—one who plays the super-silly hero and the other who plays the "serious person." As you browse through these skits, you will find that they are very adaptable to a variety of topics and situations and are easy to use. Here are just a few of the great benefits you will find in each skit:

MATCHING TOPICS

Each of the skits in this book focuses on the integrity of God's Word, but could also be used to introduce various lessons or jump-start interactive discussions. See page 6 for a list of teaching topics to match skits with stories or themes in your curriculum. See page 3 for a short synopsis of each skit. Flip to any skit to find a more detailed summary of the teaching.

CREATING CHARACTERS

Each skit provides a short synopsis of the super-silly hero. This character synopsis gives you an overview of the hero's personality and character features. The skits work best when the silliness of the hero characters is emphasized. In other words, ham it up! Keep in mind that although each hero is identified by a certain gender in this book, any character can easily be changed to match the gender of an actor. You will also find an artist's rendering of a possible low-cost, do-it-yourself costume for each hero and a list of props for each skit. Of course, feel free to improvise with the materials available to you and develop your own super-silly look. The sillier it is, the more the kids will love it.

THE SKIT AND SIDEKICKS COLUMN

The skit itself is super-silly, so have fun! Each skit has a bit of quick back-and-forth banter, and with a little practice, you will find that the dialogue flows naturally and logically.

If you like to improvise, you will love the Sidekicks column. This column gives you only the key points, so that you can easily keep the skit on track and also have the freedom to add a bit of your own personality and pizzazz to the work. There is also room for you to write your own skit notes. Feel free to duplicate the Sidekicks column and hide sections of it among your props or on a nearby podium for quick reference. Just like a hero's sidekick, it is there to help if you get in a bind.

Of course, as a final note, do not forget to make sure that the message of each skit is not lost in the hilarity. Make the teaching points clear and concise so that the children viewing the skit receive the powerful message of God's truth.

REPRODUCIBLE CLIP ART

The super-silly heroes are ready to fight villainous villains anytime you need them through reproducible illustrations at the end of each skit and on pages 79–80.

The illustration at the end of each skit includes the super-silly hero's message. These are perfect for church newsletters, bulletins, and take-home flyers. They can also be used to enhance your lessons in the classroom. Here are a few more suggestions of how to use the illustrations:

- **Trading Cards** Copy the illustrations on white card stock to create super-fun, super-silly trading cards that children can decorate, trade, and treasure! You may also want to include the lessons' memory verses on the backs of the cards as a creative way to encourage children to memorize God's Word.

- **Silly Stationery** Copy and cut out the super-silly hero illustrations and paste each one onto a corner of a blank sheet of paper. Then, copy the paper to create ready-made, super-silly hero stationery that can be used for letters to parents or children.

- **Bulletin Board** The illustrations can be enlarged and displayed on any bulletin board. Allow children to color and decorate the super-silly hero pictures.

On pages 79–80, there are smaller reproducible illustrations of all 12 super-silly heroes that are the perfect size for any project. Add your own message to create your own hero comic, use them to enhance classroom worksheets or memory verse cards, or create take-home treasures for children. (Super-silly heroes are quite versatile!) Use these illustrations anywhere to remind children of the integrity of God's Word and the message of each skit.

Here are some ideas to get you started:

- **Bookmarks** Cut out strips from card stock and cover them with thin plaid fabric. Have each child choose an illustration of her favorite hero, and then color and glue it to the front of her bookmark.

- **Reflection Pages** Decorate writing worksheets. Copy, cut out, and paste the clip art on lined paper. Then, copy the paper for each child. Encourage children to record their insights and reflections on the hero's message after each skit is presented. Collect and keep all of the reflection pages as children complete them. When children have written about all of the heroes' messages, bind each child's reflection pages together. Allow each child to use copies of the illustrations to create a collage for a cover.

- **T-Shirts, etc.** Scan the clip art into your computer and print it on iron-on transfer paper. Follow the manufacturer's instructions for applying the decals to T-shirts, caps, canvas bags, etc.

- **Stickers** Copy or scan the clip art into your computer and print it on self-adhesive labels to create your own super-silly hero stickers.

- **Super-Silly Hero Day** Plan a celebration in which everyone comes dressed as his favorite super-silly hero. Make mini-posters using the clip art illustrations and display them around the room. Decorate the room with plaid and/or polka-dot materials. Have each child share his super-silly hero's message with the class.

★ Teaching Topics ★

Super-Silly Hero Skits can be used to enhance various Bible lessons. The list below offers suggestions for matching the skits with Bible topics. Turn to the first page of each skit for an in-depth summary of the message that will help you select a super-silly hero skit that fits your needs.

1. The Inexplicable Plaidman
Moses' call to lead Israel out of Egypt
Esther
Temptation of Jesus

2. Jamma Jamma
God's people entering the Promised Land
Jonah
Jesus and the rich man

3. Polka Dot
John the Baptist
Deborah
Paul teaching Timothy

4. The Squeak
Shadrach, Meshach, and Abednego
Daniel facing the lions' den
David

5. Rewind Girl
Old Testament prophets
Paul's letters
Peter walking on water

6. Plaidman: Bionic Edition
Proverbs
Solomon
Jesus teaching as a child

7. Walkie-Talkie Woman
The Ten Commandments
Eli and Samuel

8. Engorge, Member of E.A.T.
Miracles of Jesus
Disciples filled with the Spirit
Revelations

9. The Mysterious Mind Melder-er
God's judgment through the Old
    Testament prophets
Peter's denial of Jesus
Saul's salvation

10. Chick Chameleon
Abraham and Lot
Esther
Jesus calling His disciples

11. Infomercial Guy, Guphygai Warrior
Moses and the Pharaoh
Elijah and the prophets of Baal
Jesus and the woman at the well

12. The New and Improved Infomercial Guy
Centurion believing Jesus' Word for healing
Jesus and the woman accused of sin
Salvation

★ CHARACTER

The Inexplicable Plaidman is a bumbling hero who presents himself as a campy superhero wannabe. He stands like a hero, smiles like a hero, and talks like a hero. But, he is clearly more like a cartoon character.

★ PROPS

Plaidman needs a Bible, preferably in a plaid cover so that it matches his outlandish outfit.

★ MUSIC

When Plaidman enters or exits, play music, such as *Pomp and Circumstance* or *Gonna' Fly Now* (theme from *Rocky*).

★ COSTUME CREATION

Here are some thrifty suggestions for creating your own Plaidman costume. Feel free to improvise! For this character, it is best if none of the plaid fabrics match.

MESSY HAIR
due to being too busy fighting evil with plaid

WIDE SMILE
to throw off any villainous villain

PLAID CAPE
Use plaid fabric, plaid sheet, or even a plaid skirt that has been cut in half.

PLAID SOCKS
If you can't find plaid socks—try argyle!

PLAID MASK
Glue plaid fabric to a party mask.

PLAID SHIRT
worn backward to eliminate any lines

PLAID BIBLE
Wrap a small Bible in a plaid fabric sleeve—he can't fight evil without it!

PLAID PANTS
Visit a thrift store for funky plaid pants.

PLAID FLIP-FLOPS
A superhero in flip-flops? If they're plaid, they're perfect!

GOD'S WORD WILL WORK FOR ANYONE

God is not looking for people who have great looks, big brains, or even truckloads of talent. There is nothing wrong with those things, but God looks at something more important: the heart. Every day, He looks for individuals who are available and willing to put His Word into practice. In this skit, kids will meet The Inexplicable Plaidman and discover that it doesn't matter who you are, how you look, or what talents you have—if you're willing to act on God's Word, His truth will work for you.

SIDEKICKS

L: *[begins lesson]* Is there anyone who can help?

Leader: To start off, we're going to look at a Bible verse in *[inserts any book of the Bible that might be used for today's lesson].* Let's see, is there anyone who can help me find it?

[pauses as children volunteer to help; music starts, and the door to the room flies open]

P: *[music begins; enters]*

Plaidman: *[stands in a heroic stance in the doorway with a wide smile]* Ha-ha-ha-HAAA! Did I hear a cry for help?

Leader: Um . . . I guess that was me. I was just seeing if one of these kids could help me.

P: Job for a hero!

Plaidman: *[walks with an exaggerated cowboy walk toward the leader]* Nonsense, mortal! This sounds like a job for a hero!

Leader: *[looks Plaidman up and down]* Uh-huh. Do you know one?

P: I'm a hero! *[music plays]*

Plaidman: That I do! For, I am a hero! Introducing The Inexplicable Plaidman! *[music plays again; bows and enjoys the applause]*

L: Does he look like a hero?

Leader: You're a hero? Does he look like a hero, boys and girls? *[allows responses]*

Plaidman: I know what you're thinking. You're wondering if I'm really a hero.

Leader: I just said that.

Plaidman: Exactly. I would expect that question from a mortal. To your untrained eye, I look just like anyone else in this room.

SIDEKICKS

P: What sets me
apart?

P: I fight evil with
plaid.

P: Let me show you
how it works.

L: *[Test 1]* Let's say
you go to bed and
Dark comes.

Leader: I don't know if I'd say that . . .

Plaidman: What would you say sets me apart? My sparkling
personality? My bulging muscles? My panther-like reflexes?

Leader: I'd say . . . it's the plaid.

Plaidman: So, you've discovered my secret weapon against evil!

Leader: Which is . . . ?

Plaidman: I fight evil with plaid.

Leader: With . . . plaid?

Plaidman: Precisely.

Leader: I'm not sure I understand.

Plaidman: *[rolls his eyes]* All right, let me break it down for you. Give
me a situation, and I'll show you how it works.

Leader: You'll show me how you fight evil with plaid?

Plaidman: Didn't I just say that?

Leader: This ought to be good. OK, let's say you're in bed at night
trying to fall asleep.

Plaidman: I don't go to sleep.

Leader: You don't go to sleep?

Plaidman: I'm a hero. I don't need sleep, unlike you mortals . . .

Leader: Well, let's pretend.

Plaidman: Very well.

Leader: Let's say you're in bed at night reading a book.

Plaidman: Ah, good one.

Leader: And suddenly, the Dark comes into the room.

Plaidman: I've faced him many times before. A very villainous villain.

Leader: So, what do you do so that you don't get scared?

SIDEKICKS

L: Spider!

Plaidman: I don't get scared.

Leader: There's a spider on your leg!

Plaidman: *[jumps in fear]* Aaaaaack! Get it off!

Leader: *[smiles]*

P: *[Reads 2 Timothy 1:7 KJV, personalizing it]*

Plaidman: OK, sometimes I get scared. Here's what I do. *[pulls out his plaid Bible]* I pull out my trusty Plaid Book, and I read. "God has not given me a spirit of fear, but of power and love and of a sound mind." Those words give my spirit courage, and they make the Dark cower. Understand?

Leader: I think so, but let's try another. Let's say that you just moved into a new house.

Plaidman: I'm a hero. I live in a super-plaid fortress. Why would I want to move?

Leader: Just pretend. We like pretending, don't we boys and girls? *[allows responses]*

Plaidman: *[rolls his eyes]* Mortals.

L: *[Test 2]* Let's say you move and Nervousness comes.

Leader: So, you move into a new house, and you don't know anyone on your block. Making new friends can be kind of hard. You face Nervousness.

Plaidman: Nervousness—a villainy, villainous villain.

Leader: What do you do?

P: *[Reads Joshua 1:9, personalizing it]*

Plaidman: Ah! *[holds up Bible]* Again, I start by pulling out my trusty Plaid Book. Then, I read, "I will be strong and courageous. I won't be terrified or discouraged. For the Lord my God will be with me wherever I go."

Leader: That's good advice.

Plaidman: Yes, those words will stir inside me and give me the courage that I need to step out and make new friends. They make Nervousness shrink every time.

L: *[Test 3]* Let's say you do something wrong, and Guilt comes.

Leader: Cool. Let's do one more. This time, let's pretend that you did something wrong.

Plaidman: I'm a hero. I don't do anything wrong. That's the power of plaid.

Leader: Right. Do you believe he's never made a mistake, boys and girls? *[allows responses]* Well, they're not so sure, so let's pretend that you did something wrong because everyone makes mistakes.

Plaidman: All right. We'll pretend.

Leader: So, you did something wrong, and you feel awful about it. Guilt is knocking at your door.

Plaidman: Ah, Guilt! A very villainy, villainous villain.

Leader: So, what do you do?

P: *[reads Acts 10:43, personalizing it]*

Plaidman: Once again, I use my plaid wiles, and I pull out my trusty Plaid Book. I read, "Because I believe in Jesus, my sins are forgiven through Him."

Leader: Good words.

Plaidman: Many more where that came from.

L: That's a Bible! 2 Timothy 1:7 Joshua 1:9 Acts 10:43

Leader: Wait a minute! You know what I think? I think that plaid book is a Bible! And those were three Bible verses: 2 Timothy 1:7, Joshua 1:9, and Acts 10:43.

Plaidman: *[acts irritated]* Oh sure, and next you're going to say that I'm not really a hero, but just one of the children's church leaders dressed up in a silly outfit.

Leader: Oh no, I'd never say that.

P: The Bible tells me how to be a true hero.

Plaidman: Well, you're right. This is the Bible. It contains every secret about being a true hero. It tells me how to have courage, how to stand against evil, and how to always do what's right.

L: So, you fight evil with God's Word.

Leader: So, you don't really fight evil with plaid, do you? You fight evil with the power and truth of God's Word. You just do what the Bible says.

Plaidman: Well, if you want to be technical about it . . .

SIDEKICKS

L: Anyone who uses God's Word can be a hero.

P: God's Word makes us all heroes. When evil strikes, strike back with plaid!

P: *[music plays as Plaidman leaves]*

Leader: The boys and girls and I want to know if you have any other superpowers other than the plaid?

Plaidman: *[looks around himself]* No, that's pretty much it.

Leader: Well, that's the way it should be. It just goes to prove that anyone who uses God's Word can battle evil like a hero. It doesn't matter who you are, how old you are, what you look like, or what talents you have.

Plaidman: That's right! God's Word makes us all heroes. We just have to do what it says—that's in James 1:22. Well, mortals, I must be off. I have people to save and groceries to buy. So, until next time, remember my motto: When evil strikes, strike back with plaid!

[music plays as Plaidman gallantly walks toward the door, then pauses]

By the way, that motto is trademark pending—just so you know.

Leader: Thank you, Plaidman. You're truly inexplicable.

Plaidman: Thank you, my friend. Thank you.

ANYONE WHO USES GOD'S WORD CAN BE A HERO.

★ CHARACTER

Jamma Jamma is a hero with a baby alter ego. His powers are as infantile as his beliefs about life. Ask yourself what a 30-year-old baby would look and act like, and you have just met Jamma Jamma. Softening your Rs as you talk adds a nice touch.

★ PROPS

Jamma Jamma needs a large, noisy rattle, baby blanket, pacifier, and a baby bottle. The leader needs a Bible that is bookmarked at Hebrews 5:14.

★ MUSIC

When Jamma Jamma enters or exits, play baby music, such as *Twinkle, Twinkle Little Star* or a lullaby.

★ COSTUME CREATION

Here are some thrifty suggestions for creating your own Jamma Jamma costume. Feel free to improvise! For this character, anything babyish is perfect.

RATTLE
a must for this super-silly hero—the larger the better!

BABY BONNET
Use a strip of pink or blue fabric to create a bonnet.

BIB
Use construction paper to cut out the letters "PJ" for the bib—like a hero's emblem.

MUSTACHE
adds to the silliness of the adult/baby contradiction

PACIFIER
What baby would be without a pacifier?

PAJAMAS
nightgown or footed pajamas—anything frilly and babyish

BABY BLANKET
Jamma's "blankie" is his shield.

BABY BOOTIES
Fuzzy socks or slippers would also work.

BABY BOTTLE
filled with water or juice

Growing Up with the Word

When you become a Christian, your life changes completely. You think differently, act differently, and you have a new outlook on life—both eternally and for the here and now. The feeling is so wonderful that it is easy to wallow in it, becoming stagnant in the bliss of a new life. However, God desires that we do not stop with the new birth. He wants us to continue growing in Him, discovering new things, and reaching beyond our comfort zones into the lost world around us. In this skit, kids will meet Jamma Jamma and find out that God has a plan for each of us to grow in our faith, to become stronger, and to move from the "milk" of the Word to the "meat."

SIDEKICKS

L: [begins lesson as usual]	**Leader:**	OK everybody, next we're going to . . .
J: [cries from out of sight]	**Jamma:**	[cries from out of sight] Waaaaaahhhh!
	Leader:	Er . . . as I was saying, next we're going to . . .
	Jamma:	[cries from out of sight again] Waaaaaahhhh!
L: Who's crying?	**Leader:**	[addresses the kids; acts concerned] Is everyone all right? Who's crying? [plays this up, goes from kid-to-kid] Is it you?
J: [enters] It's me!	**Jamma:**	[bursts into the room] It's meeeeee! Waaaaaahhhh!
	Leader:	Oh, my! And, who are you?
J: I'm a hero.	**Jamma:**	[walks to front of room] My name is Jamma Jamma. I'm a hero! But, you can call me P. J.
	Leader:	You're a hero? Really?
J: This may look like a regular rattle.	**Jamma:**	Don't let my infantile nature fool you. I actually have quite a few tricks. For instance, this may look like a regular rattle, but it's not!
L: What does it do?	**Leader:**	What does it do?
	Jamma:	[shakes rattle]
	Leader:	[looks dubiously at audience]
	Jamma:	Getting sleepy?

SIDEKICKS

J: I think I grabbed the wrong rattle.

L: Does your blanket do anything?

J: Hit me.

L: You're a hero with superpowers. You have to be *ready*?

Leader: No.

Jamma: *[shakes rattle again; looks confused]* Oh, man! I think I grabbed the wrong rattle. Anyway, I have one of these back in my crib that will put any villain to sleep, instantly! Works faster than a talk radio show.

Leader: *[yawns as if bored]*

Jamma: Aha! It *is* working!

Leader: *[perks up and looks wide awake]* So, tell me, does your blanket do anything?

Jamma: *[eyes widen as he whips blanket off his shoulder]* My blankie? Yeah! Try and hit me.

Leader: I'm not going to hit you.

Jamma: Chicken?

Leader: No, I just don't . . . hit babies.

Jamma: *[speaks childishly]* I'm not a baby! You're a baby!

Leader: I'm a baby?

Jamma: I know you are, but what am I?

Leader: A . . . *big* baby?

Jamma: I know you are, but what am I?

Leader: *[hits Jamma playfully on the arm]*

Jamma: *[whines]* Hey, you hit me!

Leader: You told me to!

Jamma: I wasn't ready!

Leader: But, you're a hero with superpowers . . . do you have to be *ready*?

Jamma: Well . . . sometimes . . . I wanna' do-over!

SIDEKICKS

L and J: *[playfully go back and forth hitting and trying to block the hits with blanket. Finally, Jamma throws blanket over leader's head.]*

Leader: *[hits Jamma playfully on the other arm]*

Jamma: *[swings to block the hit with his blanket, but misses; leader hits him on the other arm, and Jamma misses again; repeat several times. Each time Jamma swings the blanket, he shouts]* Goo-ga! Goo-goo-ga-ga!
[Finally, he throws the blanket over the leader's head.]

Leader: *[stands perfectly still for a moment]* You got me. *[pulls blanket off head]*

Jamma: That's the power of the blankie. Now, if you were really a bad guy, I'd launch my pacifier at you, too.

Leader: Oh, really?

Jamma: Yeah! Want to see?

L: It's time we get back to our lesson. You could join us or go to the nursery.

Leader: No, no. Keep your pacifier right where it is. Now, if that's all, it's time we get back to our lesson. Why don't you go have a seat, or if you'd rather, we can send you to the nursery. *[nudges Jamma Jamma toward the door]*

J: *[cries]*

Jamma: *[bursts into tears]* Waaaaaahhhh!

Leader: Oh, my! I'm sorry. I was just kidding. You can stay in here.

Jamma: *[sniffs]* No, it's not that.

Leader: What is it then?

J: Why does everyone treat me like a big baby?

Jamma: Why is it that everywhere I go . . . *[blows nose loudly into blanket]* Why is it that everyone always treats me like a big baby?

Leader: *[addresses class]* Um . . . does anyone out there have any ideas? *[takes a few answers—someone will surely say it's because he looks like a big baby. If not, submit that suggestion yourself.]* We think it might be because you kind of *look* like a big baby.

Jamma: *[pouts]* Even the other heroes make fun of me. No one takes me seriously.

L: Maybe it's time to grow up.

Leader: Well, friend, maybe it's time to grow up.

SIDEKICKS

J: Grow up?

Jamma: *[fearfully]* Grow up?! But . . . but . . . but . . . if I grow up, I'll have to eat solid foods! I'll have to dress myself! *[gasps]* I'd have to learn to use the potty!

Leader: *[nods]* That you will.

Jamma: It all seems so . . . so . . . *hard.*

L: Think of everything that will get better.

Leader: Maybe, but think of everything that will get better. If you're hungry, you won't have to cry until someone feeds you. You can pick out your own clothes. And you won't have to sit around in dirty diapers until someone notices.

Jamma: Hmm, there are perks. *[looks almost convinced]*

L: The same thing happens when you become a Christian.

Leader: The same thing happens when you become a Christian.

Jamma: How's that?

L: When you become a Christian, you're a baby in Christ.

Leader: Well, when you become a Christian, you're like a baby in Christ. You know a few things about living for Jesus—like that you shouldn't lie or steal—but there's so much more to learn and experience.

Jamma: Like what?

L: We have to become more mature in God. It's the solid food of our faith.

Leader: Like getting to know God by reading the Bible, *[holds up a Bible]* praying, and sharing Jesus with others. They're all part of becoming more mature in God. These things are the "solid food" of our faith.

Jamma: *[nods in understanding and holds out baby bottle]* Oh . . . you have to be mature to eat solid food.

L: *[opens Bible]* Hebrews 5:14 says that God has solid faith food for us.

Leader: *[opens Bible]* Hebrews 5:14 says just that. God has solid faith food for us when we're ready to handle it.

J: I'm ready now!

Jamma: *[hops up and down excitedly]* I'm ready! I'm ready! I'm ready! I want it now!

L: Even Jesus had to grow up in faith.

Leader: It doesn't all happen at once. Spend time with God, spend time in church, and spend time reading the Bible, and you'll grow more mature in your faith every day. Even Jesus had to do those things.

SIDEKICKS

L: Luke 2:52 says that Jesus grew in wisdom and stature and in favor with God and men.

L: We'll see you soon. Let's get on with our lesson.

J: *[leaves]*

Jamma: Jesus had to grow up in faith?

Leader: Luke 2:52 says that when Jesus was young, He grew in wisdom and stature and in favor with God and men.

Jamma: Wow! I'll go ask my parents if I can stay. *[starts to leave]*

Leader: Great, we'll see you soon. *[turns to class]* OK, so let's get on with the lesson.

Jamma: *[suddenly stops and holds his stomach]* Ewww. Ow. Wait a second.

Leader: What's wrong?

Jamma: *[acts relieved]* I'm OK now. For a minute there, I thought I needed to be burped.

Leader: *[shakes head and waves]* Bye, Jamma Jamma.

Jamma: Bye-bye!

GOD'S WORD IS THE "SOLID FOOD" OF OUR FAITH.

★ CHARACTER

Polka Dot presents herself as larger-than-life, following the example of her mentor, The Inexplicable Plaidman. She is younger though, and it shows by the young and hip way that she talks and carries herself.

★ PROPS

Polka Dot has a Bible, just like The Inexplicable Plaidman, except it's covered with polka dots instead of plaid. Bookmark Polka Dot's Bible at Hebrews 11.

★ MUSIC

Play loud polka music when Polka Dot enters or exits.

★ COSTUME CREATION

Here are some thrifty suggestions for creating your own Polka Dot costume. Feel free to improvise! For this character, it's best if none of the polka-dot fabrics match.

POLKA-DOT BIBLE Wrap a small Bible with polka-dot fabric. Skit notes may be hidden inside.

POLKA-DOT MASK Glue polka-dot fabric or paper to a party mask

POLKA-DOT BELT multiple belts or polka-dot scarf

POLKA-DOT DRESS skirt, blouse, or even polka-dot pants

POLKA-DOT TIGHTS/LEGGINGS the bolder, the better

MESSY PIGTAILS just like Plaidman—too busy fighting villains to fix her hair

WIDE SMILE shows she young, hip, and happy in polka dots

POLKA-DOT CAPE use polka-dot fabric or a sheet, or cut a polka-dot skirt in half

POLKA-DOT SLIPPERS decorate slippers with stickers or markers

HEROES IN THE WORD

The Bible is jam-packed with stories about ordinary people doing extraordinary things with God. From the first to the last story, readers clearly see that biblical heroes are just regular people taking God at His Word. In this skit, Polka Dot, The Inexplicable Plaidman's understudy, discovers that the Bible is not only filled with great examples of heroes, but it is also the ultimate measure of whether someone is a true hero.

NOTE: Most skits in this book can stand alone, but this skit needs to occur sometime after The Inexplicable Plaidman skit to be fully enjoyed.

SIDEKICKS

L: *[begins lesson as usual]* Can anyone help me find my Bible?	**Leader:** For today's lesson—it's going to be a fun one—we're going to look at a Bible verse and . . . oh, wait . . . I think I left my Bible at the back of the room. Can anyone help me find it? *[pauses as children volunteer to help, polka music starts and the door to the room flies open]*
P: *[polka music plays; enters]*	**Polka Dot:** *[stands in a heroic stance in the doorway with a wide smile]* Hee-hee-hee-HEEE! Did I hear a cry for help?
	Leader: Wow. Well, actually, everything is OK. I just forgot my Bible. It's back there on the table. *[points to the back of the room]*
P: Job for a hero! *[polka music plays again]*	**Polka Dot:** Nonsense, mortal! This sounds like a job for a hero! *[polka music plays again as she runs over, grabs the Bible, and then polka shuffles to the music toward the leader]*
	Leader: We seem to be overrun by heroes lately. Are you telling me that you're a hero, too?
P: I'm Polka Dot!	**Polka Dot:** Yes, mortal! I'm Polka Dot! *[does a little polka dance]*
	Leader: You know, you kind of remind me of someone. Does she remind you of someone, boys and girls? *[allows responses]*
	Polka Dot: You guys are smart. Yes, some people say I look like The Inexplicable Plaidman. Do you remember him?
	Leader: He's kind of hard to forget.

SIDEKICKS

P: Plaidman is my mentor. I want to be just like him.

L: You mean by putting the Word into practice?

L: Your Bible is like Plaidman's, too.

P: I'm kind of like a big fish with spots on its body.

Polka Dot: What a compliment! I hope I'm hard to forget, too.

Leader: I can almost guarantee it.

Polka Dot: I hope that one day I'm as inexplicable as Plaidman. He's my mentor, you know.

Leader: No kidding?

Polka Dot: *[folds her hands in front of her heart like a little girl]* Yes! I adore Plaidman. He's my hero, and I want to be used by God just like he is. That's why I try to do everything just like he does.

Leader: You mean like fighting evil with the Word of God? Plaidman showed us how he put the Word into practice by quoting Bible verses and living by them.

Polka Dot: *[silent for a long moment]*

Leader: What?

Polka Dot: *[says with wide-eyed wonder]* You are so deep.

Leader: *[points to Polka Dot's Bible]* Hey, you've even got a Bible like Plaidman's.

Polka Dot: *[holds Bible up]* Yeah, but mine's polka-dotted instead of plaid. *[points to costume]* I've also got a cape like him, a mask like him, and hero slippers like his, except everything I have is polka-dotted.

Leader: I noticed.

Polka Dot: I thought about doing the plaid, but then, I thought the polka dots might set me apart.

Leader: They do. Believe me.

Polka Dot: I'm kind of like one of those fish with big spots on its body. When predators approach, my disguise automatically fools them into thinking that I have a thousand big eyes all over my body, and they're like, "Eeek! A mammoth fishy!" And, they run because no one likes a big fish.

Leader: *[silent for a long moment]*

Polka Dot: What?

Leader: You are so deep.

Polka Dot: Thank you. I owe it all to Plaidman.

L: We all need mentors—people we can learn from.

Leader: That's great! We all need good mentors in our lives. You know, good examples we can learn from.

Polka Dot: *[acts worried]* You can't have Plaidman. He's already taken, and his schedule is full.

Leader: Oh no, I'm not trying to steal him from you. I'm just saying that we all need to find someone who sets a good example that we can follow.

Polka Dot: Yeah, but too bad for you. I don't know if there's anyone else out there who's as good as Plaidman.

Leader: Well, there's no one quite like Plaidman, but there are a lot of good people out there. Can I see your Bible? *[Polka Dot hands over her Bible.]*

L: *[looks at Hebrews 11 for examples of Bible heroes; refers to Hebrews 11:39]*

Look in Hebrews 11, for example. Does anyone have a Bible who can look with me?

[interacts with the kids, having them point out the names of people in the chapter]

It shows that since the beginning of time, there have been people who have set great examples to follow. Now, look at verse 39. It says that they were all commended for their faith. So, we should look at their lives and see how they lived.

Polka Dot: Yeah, but they all made mistakes.

Leader: Sure, but they did a lot of things right, too. The mark of a good mentor is someone who rights his wrongs.

Polka Dot: *[stares wide-eyed at leader]*

L: Jesus is the best example of all.

Leader: What? *[pauses]* Oh, yeah. You said I was deep. *[pauses again]* And, don't forget Jesus. He's the best example of all. He always did what God wanted Him to do, without fail. *[hands Bible back to Polka Dot]*

SIDEKICKS

P: The Bible is our ultimate mentor.

Polka Dot: So, the Bible tells us exactly how to live right? It's like our ultimate mentor?

Leader: That's right! When you look at someone's life, compare it to what the Bible says to see if he is living for Jesus. If he has joy, peace, integrity, and love for God, then he might just measure up to the Word's definition of a good example.

P: God's Word is a like measuring stick.

Polka Dot: *[holds the Bible lengthwise in front of her eyes]* It's like a measuring stick.

Leader: Yeah, a ruler.

Polka Dot: *[snickers]*

Leader: What?

Polka Dot: God's Word rules! Ha! Get it? It rules! It's a ruler!

Leader: *[smiles]* Pun intended.

Polka Dot: Well, I have to tell you, this sure takes a load off my mind.

Leader: How's that?

P: Plaidman is a good example of someone who follows God.

Polka Dot: Just everything we talked about proves that I've made the right choice. Plaidman is a great example of someone who's following God, so I can learn a lot from him.

Leader: That's good to hear.

Polka Dot: Yeah, well . . . you know, it's a good thing because—between you and me, mortal—he's really not that talented.

Leader: You don't say.

P: It's two polka-dot freckles past a hair.

Polka Dot: *[looks at her wrist]* Well, look at the time. It's two polka-dot freckles past a hair. Gotta' get back to work. Can't let the bad guys run the streets now, can we?

Leader: I think it's safe to say we'll all feel better knowing you're out there.

Polka Dot: That's good to hear! Now, everyone stand up. Strike up the music, maestro!

SIDEKICKS

P: *[Polka shuffles to the music toward the exit.]* It doesn't matter who you are or what you look like—God can use you!

Polka Dot: *[polka music starts; shuffles down the aisle and interacts with children along the way; pauses at the door; music stops]* Remember, it doesn't matter who you are, what you look like, or what talents you have. As long as you're available— and ready to learn—God can use you!

Leader: Thank you, Polka Dot!

Polka Dot: Anytime! And, if you ever need help, just polka! *[shuffles out the door]*

Leader: *[laughs]* Did she just say if we ever need help, we should just . . . *polka?*

GOD'S WORD RULES!

★ CHARACTER

The Squeak is a young whippersnapper who wants to become a full-fledged hero no matter what it takes. He's energetic and enthusiastic—and a bit on the nerdy side.

★ PROPS

The Squeak needs black-framed glasses; a pocket protector holding pens and pencils (keep glasses and pocket protector hidden until cued in the script); and small squeak toys, such as rubber ducks or bike horns, stuffed into pockets. The leader needs a Bible that is bookmarked at Matthew 6:33.

★ COSTUME CREATION

Here are some thrifty suggestions for creating your own Squeak costume. Of course, feel free to improvise!

BLACK TURBAN
Wrap a piece of black cloth or a black winter scarf around your head.

GLASSES
black-framed novelty glasses—the nerdier, the better

BLACK SHIRT
with front chest pocket

POCKET PROTECTOR
filled with pens and pencils

LONG, FLOWING BLACK CAPE
big enough to wrap around yourself—like a bedsheet

BLACK PANTS WITH PLENTY OF POCKETS
for holding squeak toys, pocket protector, script, glasses, etc.

HIDDEN SQUEAK TOYS
under armpits, inside shirt or pockets

BLACK SHOES
White socks and black dress shoes would be hilarious.

Putting the Word First

People are always looking for quick fixes to make life easier. We frequently fall for "free" offers and anything that looks like it might help us earn fast cash. But God has a different plan in mind for us—seek Him, above all else, and then, whatever you truly need will fall into place. In this skit, The Squeak learns that seeking God is the only way to total fulfillment and a truly rich life.

SIDEKICKS

L: *[begins lesson; hears squeaking noise from back of room]*

Leader: Today's lesson is all about . . . *[squeaking sound comes from the back of the room]* Did you hear that? *[more squeaking until the kids realize where it's coming from]*

S: *[enters]*

Squeak: Hey, there! Ho, there! Hi, there!

Leader: *[acts startled]* Why, hello there! Welcome to our church! If I didn't know better, I'd say that you were a hero of some kind.

S: I'm almost a hero.

Squeak: *[squeaks twice more and walks to front of room]* Aw, you made me blush! But yes, I'm The Squeak, hero extraordinaire! Well, I'm almost a hero anyway.

Leader: Almost a hero?

S: I'm just a sidekick right now.

Squeak: *[squeaks twice]* Well, you can't just become a hero overnight, you know. I'm just a sidekick right now. But, I'm on my way. See, I've got a cape. *[holds cape out in an exaggerated superhero stance]*

Leader: It's very nice.

S: I can also run very fast.

Squeak: *[squeaks twice]* Thank you. I can also run very fast. *[runs very fast in place]*

Leader: That was pretty fast.

Squeak: *[squeaks twice]* And, I have X-ray vision.

Leader: You do?

SIDEKICKS

Squeak: *[squeaks twice]* Yep! *[looks at class and then starts snickering]*

Leader: What?

Squeak: *[squeaks twice; still snickering]* One of the kids out there has a lizard in his pocket.

Leader: *[looks stunned and then shakes head]* I don't think you really have X-ray vision.

Squeak: *[squeaks twice]* Well, I have 20/20 vision anyway.

Leader: Say, what's with all the squeaking?

S: Important part of being a hero is doing what the Bible says.

Squeak: *[squeaks twice]* Ah, well, that's the most important part of being a hero, in my humble opinion. You have to do what the Bible says.

L: Why squeaking?

Leader: That's true. Following the Bible is the most important part of being a hero. But, what does that have to do with squeaking?

Squeak: *[squeaks twice]* I thought you'd know that since you teach in a church. It's right there in the Bible as plain as day. You don't need X-ray vision to see it.

Leader: You lost me.

S: Matthew 6:33—says to *squeak* God.

Squeak: *[squeaks twice]* Matthew 6:33 says, *[squeaks twice]* "Squeak the Kingdom of God above all else!"

Leader: Is that what Matthew 6:33 says, boys and girls? *[allows responses]*

Squeak: *[squeaks once]* I'm wrong?

L: I think you misread it. It says . . .

Leader: I think you misread it. It says . . .

Squeak: I didn't misread it.

Leader: I think you did.

Squeak: I couldn't have. I didn't read it. I heard someone say it.

Leader: Well, then you misheard it.

S: Give me a clue as to what it says.

Squeak: Yes, that's more likely. But, don't tell me! I should know this! I know what it's supposed to be! *[pauses and concentrates hard]* OK, I need a clue.

L: It rhymes with *squeak.*

Leader: Well, the word you're looking for rhymes with *squeak.*

Squeak: Oh! I've got it! *[tiptoes and sneaks around the room]*

Leader: Um . . . what are you doing?

S: Sneak?

Squeak: *[still tiptoeing]* I'm *sneaking* the Kingdom of God above all else!

Leader: No, it's not *sneak* the kingdom either. *Sneak* isn't the right word.

Squeak: *[still tiptoeing]* It's not *sneak*?

Leader: No.

S: Sleep?

Squeak: *[stops tiptoeing]* Good. My toes were starting to hurt. Oh! I've got it. *[suddenly drops to the floor, closes eyes and wraps cape around himself in a single swoop]*

Leader: Now, what are you doing?

Squeak: *[whispers]* I'm *sleeping* the Kingdom of God above all else!

Leader: Sleeping! That's not what it says either!

S: Peek?

Squeak: *[jumps up, covers his face with hands and then opens them to look at the leader]* Peek the Kingdom of God above all else?

Leader: No!

S: *[pulls out glasses and pocket protector]* Geek?

Squeak: *[thinks for a moment; pulls a pair of glasses out of a pocket and puts them on; pulls out pocket protector holding pens and pencils and puts it in his shirt pocket]* Geek the Kingdom of God above all else!

Leader: *Geek* the Kingdom of God? What does that even mean?

Squeak: *[looks dejected]* I'm trying very hard.

Leader: I can tell. Is he even close, boys and girls? *[allows responses]*

SIDEKICKS

S: Reek?

L: *[gets answer from kids]*

L: *[reads Matthew 6:33 NLT]*

S: You mean, look for Him? Is He missing?

L: *Seek* means to get to know Him better.

Squeak: Oh, no.

Leader: What?

Squeak: Please, no.

Leader: *[slightly impatient]* What?

Squeak: Please tell me it's not *reek* the Kingdom of God above all else! I don't want to reek!

Leader: Reek? You mean "to smell badly?" No, God doesn't tell us that we have to smell badly to get to know Him better.

Squeak: Whew! I was a little concerned. I like my bubble baths.

Leader: Can I give you one more clue?

Squeak: Yes, OK. One more clue.

Leader: OK. What's the answer, boys and girls? *[allows responses]*

Squeak: *[acts overly surprised]* Oh! Why didn't I think of that? How could I have missed it?

Leader: So, there you go.

Squeak: Um . . . one thing.

Leader: Yes?

Squeak: What'd they say? Too many of them were speaking at once.

Leader: *[laughs]* They said that you have to *seek* the Kingdom of God above all else. That's what Matthew 6:33 says. *[opens Bible and reads]* "Seek the Kingdom of God above all else, and live righteously, and He will give you everything you need."

Squeak: You mean look for him? *[turns to kids]* Excuse me? May I have your attention? Has anyone out there seen God? I think He's missing. Check under your chairs, please.

Leader: No, no. Don't be silly. God is always right here with us. When the Bible says that we need to *seek* God, it means that we need to find ways to get to know Him better.

SIDEKICKS

L: Seek God by praying, going to church, and reading your Bible.

Squeak: *[looks confused]* How can we do that?

Leader: We need to pray every day, go to church, and—are you ready for this?—*read* our Bibles. We shouldn't just listen to others talk about the Bible.

Squeak: Well, that would have eliminated a lot of confusion now, wouldn't it?

Leader: But, hey, the good news is, you don't need all of that stuff. You can get rid of the pocket protector *[takes it off Squeak]*, the glasses *[takes them off Squeak]*, and especially the squeakers!

S: *[drops squeak toys]*

Squeak: *[takes out the squeak toys, squeaks each one once, and drops them on the floor]* They were a little annoying.

Leader: And now, you're one step closer to being a true hero.

S: *[leaves]*

Squeak: You bet I am! *[heads to the door]* I'm going to go read my Bible and start seeking God now!

Leader: *[picks up a squeak toy and squeaks it twice]* Bye-bye!

SEEK THE KINGDOM OF GOD ABOVE ALL ELSE.

30

★ CHARACTER

Rewind Girl is a sweet, unassuming hero with a kind and giving heart. She hopes to become a better hero every day, through not only developing her own abilities, but also through developing her faith. She is upbeat, energetic, and a bit dramatic!

★ PROPS

Rewind Girl needs a TV or DVD remote control. The leader needs a Bible that is bookmarked at Romans 10:17 and Joshua 1:8.

★ COSTUME CREATION

Here are some thrifty suggestions for creating your own Rewind Girl costume. Feel free to improvise! Gather old VHS cassette or audio cassette tapes. Pull out the film and cut it into long strips to use for this costume.

BLACK MASK
What's a super-silly hero without a mask?

REMOTE CONTROL
to help with her rewinding superpower

CASSETTE TAPE-ACCENTED SLEEVES
VHS, cassette, or other type of film strips wrapped around shirt sleeves

BLACK TIGHTS OR LEGGINGS
adds to the effect!

SHINY BLACK SHOES
to match the cassette film

CASSETTE TAPE HAIR
Make a wig out of VHS or other type of film strips and hold in place with a headband.
Cut out the letter R from construction paper and glue to front of headband.

CASSETTE TAPE CAPE
Use shiny black material or a large, plastic leaf bag. Or, glue pieces of cassette film to any piece of fabric.

CASSETTE TAPE SKIRT OR PANTS
Drape strips of film from a black skirt or pants—think hula skirt!

FAITH COMES FROM HEARING THE WORD

All of us have a measure of faith in our hearts. But, how do we strengthen that faith? Through trying harder? Hoping more? No, faith comes from hearing God's Word. The promises in His Word that are spoken into our hearts encourage us, strengthen us, and make our faith unshakable. In this skit, kids will meet Rewind Girl, who finds out that hearing God's Word over and over again gives her faith real strength.

SIDEKICKS

L: *[begins lesson as usual]*	**Leader:** Today we're going to talk about . . . *[looks through papers]* well, let's see if I can remember . . .
R: *[enters]*	**Rewind:** *[appears at the back of the room, standing confidently with hands on hips]* Perhaps I can help!
	Leader: *[looks startled]* Oh! Who are you?
R: My superpower is that I can remember anything.	**Rewind:** *[walks to the front of the room]* I am Rewind Girl! I'm a hero, and my superpower is that I have excellent recall. I can remember anything.
L: What was your name?	**Leader:** You can remember anything, huh? What was your name again?
R: *[rewinds and plays the opening scene again]*	**Rewind:** Let me rewind and remind you! *[holds out a remote control and pushes a button; does everything she just did in superfast speed in reverse; makes rewinding sounds—like the sound of rewinding a song; once at the back of the room, she stops and perfectly replays everything that just happened]* Perhaps I can help! *[runs to front of room and changes voice to be like the leader]* Oh! Who are you? *[runs to the back of the room; walks up the aisle and changes back to her own voice]* I am Rewind Girl! I'm a hero, and my superpower is that I have excellent recall. I can remember anything. *[turns and changes voice to be like the leader again]*

SIDEKICKS

	You can remember anything, huh? Wow. What was your name again? *[changes back to her own voice]* Let me rewind and remind you!
L: Stop!	**Leader:** Wait! Stop! You don't have to rewind again. I got it that time.
	Rewind: Whew! Good. I could have gotten stuck in an infinite loop there. If you ever see that happen, just say, "Stop!" and it'll bring me back to the present time.
	Leader: Cool. So, you're like a human TiVo or a DVD.
R: I got this way chasing my arch villain, BetaMax.	**Rewind:** *[purses lips]* Well, more like a videotape. I got this way when I was chasing my arch villain, BetaMax, one day. He kept throwing old videotapes in my way as he ran from me. I tripped over them and bumped my head.
	Leader: Bumped your head? Ouch. That must have been awful.
R: *[replays chasing Betamax]*	**Rewind:** I think it was. Let's see. Rewind! *[pushes the remote; makes rewinding sounds; stops; acts as though she's running and leaping over things in her way]* Stop, BetaMax, you villainous villain! Stop this instant! *[pretends to trip, fall, and bump her head on the floor]* Owwww!
	Leader: OK, stop! Come back to the present.
	Rewind: *[jumps up]* Whew! I really got a bump on my ol' noggin. After that, public opinion of BetaMax ruined his career of villainy. Now, I'm eternally the go-to gal for memory recall.
	Leader: Still, that's quite an amazing superpower that you got from that experience. And, you put a villain out of work.
R: People don't like to rewind anymore.	**Rewind:** It's true! Though, I'm not as popular as I once was. People don't want to be kind and rewind anymore. They want instant gratification. To them, rewinding is "old school."
	Leader: Yes, I suppose that's true.
	Rewind: *[sighs]*
	Leader: And yet, I imagine that your superpower still serves you well.

SIDEKICKS

R: It's nice to be able to remember special times.

L: Like a good birthday party.

L: You might remember a fun car trip with your family.

L: Can you remember the day you were born?

L: That power can help you build your faith, too.

Rewind: I like it sometimes. It's nice to be able to remember special times in my life with absolute clarity.

Leader: Oh! Like remembering a really good birthday party.

Rewind: Yes! *[pushes the remote; makes rewinding sounds; stops; pretends to enter a house holding a full bag of groceries]*

Hey, Mom! I'm home! I have the eggs. Where is everybody?

[switches sides and yells] SURPRISE!

[switches back to where she was standing and screams in surprise; throws imaginary grocery bag in the air; watches it go up and then fall back down; grimaces when it hits the ground]

Leader: Stop! *[laughs]* You might remember the last time you went on a fun car trip with your family.

Rewind: Absolutely! *[pushes the remote; makes rewinding sounds; stops; pretends to be sitting in a car, sleeping]*

Zzzzzz . . . *[wakes up groggy]* What's that smell? *[takes a deep sniff and then suddenly is wide awake; holds nose]* Ugh! Mom! Billy took off his shoe and put it in my face again! Ugh! It stinks!

Leader: *[laughs]* OK, stop. Can you remember the day you were born?

Rewind: *[pushes the remote; makes rewinding sounds, drops to the floor and waves hands and feet in the air, crying loudly]* Waaaahh! Waaaahh! *[whimpers]* I'm hungry!

Leader: That's amazing. OK, stop!

Rewind: *[jumps up]* Cool, huh?

Leader: Sure is! I think you should be proud to be a hero with that power.

Rewind: Yes, I am. *[looks proud of herself]*

Leader: In fact, that power can help you build your faith, too.

Rewind: Rewinding can build my faith?

SIDEKICKS

	Leader: Sure, in two ways. Whenever God does something in my life, I try to remember those blessings as often as I can. It helps me to remember how good God is to me. For you, remembering that would be a snap!
	Rewind: You're right! What's the other way?
L: *[reads Romans 10:17 NLT]*	**Leader:** *[opens Bible]* Romans 10:17 says, "Faith comes from hearing, that is, hearing the Good News about Christ." In short, faith comes when you hear the Word of God.
R: *[rewinds and replays Romans 10:17]*	**Rewind:** That's good! Say that again—no wait, let me do it for you. *[pushes the remote; makes rewinding sounds and imitates the leader's voice]* Romans 10:17 says, "Faith comes from hearing, that is, hearing the Good News about Christ." In short, faith comes when you hear the Word of God. *[pushes the remote; makes rewinding sounds again]* Faith comes when you hear the Word of God.
	Leader: Stop! Yes, that's it.
	Rewind: I like hearing God's Word. Every time I hear it, my faith becomes stronger because I hear God's promises to me.
L: You can read a promise, then rewind and hear it again.	**Leader:** Exactly. You can read a promise and then rewind to hear it again and again!
R: *[looks up Joshua 1:8]*	**Rewind:** Let me see your Bible. *[takes Bible and opens it]* Here's a promise. God says in Joshua 1:8 that if I meditate on His Word day and night and do what it says, I'll be prosperous and successful!
	Leader: Yes, now rewind!
R: *[rewinds and says Joshua 1:18 twice more]*	**Rewind:** *[pushes the remote; makes rewinding sounds]* God says in Joshua 1:8 that if I meditate on His Word day and night and do what it says, I'll be prosperous and successful! *[pushes the remote; makes rewinding sounds again]* God says in Joshua 1:8 that if I meditate on His Word day and night and do what it says, I'll be prosperous and successful!
	Leader: Stop! Isn't that cool?
	Rewind: How did you know to read from the Bible like that?

SIDEKICKS

L: God wants us to meditate on His Word.

Leader: I do that myself. To strengthen my faith, I read God's promises in His Word and then remind myself of them by saying them aloud or thinking about them. That's what the word *meditate* means in that verse. God wants us to do that.

R: Everyone has this superpower!

Rewind: *[hands the Bible back]* Well, you've convinced me. I guess this superpower is something that everyone has—to a degree.

Leader: That's right.

Rewind: Well, I'm going to go start reading and rewinding!

Leader: Sounds good. Anytime you need encouragement, just remember what we talked about here today.

R: I can just rewind from the beginning.

Rewind: Oh! That'll be easy! I can just rewind to the very beginning *[pushes the remote; makes rewinding sounds; runs to back of room]* Perhaps I can help! *[runs to front of room and changes voice to be like the leader]* Oh! Who are you? *[runs to the back of room; walks up the aisle and changes back to her own voice]* I'm Rewind Girl! I'm a hero, and my superpower is that I have excellent recall. I can remember anything.
[turns and changes voice to be like the leader again]
You can remember anything, huh? Wow. What was your name again?
[changes back to her own voice] Let me rewind and remind you!

Leader: Stop! Stop! Stop!

R: When you read the Word, be kind and rewind! *[exits]*

Rewind: Whew! Thanks. I better get going now. Just remember kids, when you read God's Word, be kind and rewind!

WHEN YOU READ GOD'S WORD, BE KIND AND REWIND!

★ CHARACTER

He's back—as lovable and inexplicable as ever. The Inexplicable Plaidman is a bumbling hero who presents himself as a campy superhero wannabe. He stands like a hero, smiles like a hero, and talks like a hero. But, he is clearly more like a cartoon character. In this skit, Plaidman reveals his new super-silly power, but is it really "bionic"?

★ PROPS

Plaidman needs a Bible, preferably in a plaid cover so that it matches his outlandish outfit. Bookmark Plaidman's Bible at Psalm 119:105 and James 1:22.

★ MUSIC

When Plaidman enters or exits, play music, such as *Pomp and Circumstance* or *Gonna' Fly Now* (theme from *Rocky*).

★ COSTUME CREATION

Here are some thrifty suggestions for creating your own Plaidman costume. Feel free to improvise! For this character, it is best if none of the plaid fabrics match.

MESSY HAIR
due to being too busy fighting evil with plaid

PLAID MASK
Glue plaid fabric to a party mask.

WIDE SMILE
to throw off any villainous villain

PLAID SHIRT
worn backward to eliminate any lines

PLAID CAPE
Use plaid fabric, plaid sheet, or even a plaid skirt that has been cut in half.

PLAID BIBLE
Wrap a small Bible in a plaid fabric sleeve—he can't fight evil without it!

PLAID PANTS
Visit a thrift store for funky plaid pants.

PLAID SOCKS
If you can't find plaid socks—try argyle!

PLAID FLIP-FLOPS
A superhero in flip-flops? If they're plaid, they're perfect!

GUIDANCE FROM THE WORD

God's Word is rich and powerful, and when we face questions in life, the Bible has the answers. Sometimes, we learn those answers directly from the text; other times, we learn them from the stories of heroes in the Word. Regardless, God's Word has exactly the answers that we need every time. In this skit, The Inexplicable Plaidman returns and finds out that when questions arise, even for heroes, God's Word has all of the answers.

SIDEKICKS

L: [begins lesson as usual]

Leader: OK, let's all open our Bibles to [inserts the verse that will be used for the day's lesson] Who would like to help?

[pauses as children volunteer to help; music starts, and the door to the room flies open]

P: [music begins; enters]

Plaidman: [stands in a heroic stance in the doorway with a wide smile] Ha-ha-ha-HAAA! Did I hear a cry for help?

Leader: [unenthusiastically] Oh, look. It's The Inexplicable Plaidman.

Plaidman: [walks toward the leader with an exaggerated cowboy walk] Hello, mortal! Did I hear a cry for help? If it's a hero you need, a hero is what you've got!

Leader: [looks Plaidman up and down] Is one coming?

Plaidman: That joke never gets old, does it?

Leader: [laughing] No, not really.

P: I've taken the next step in my life as a hero.

Plaidman: But, the joke is on you, mortal! For I have taken the next step in my life as a hero.

Leader: What's that?

P: I've never had any superpowers.

Plaidman: Well, you probably never realized it, but the truth is, I've never really had any superpowers.

Leader: I thought that you fought evil with plaid.

Plaidman: That was more of just a catchphrase, really. It was big with the kids and sold thousands of action figures. But in real life, well, those were merely words.

SIDEKICKS

L: So, now you have real superpower?

P: I have bionic inserts in my shoes.

P: *[explains his bionic shoes]*

L: Show us.

P: I ran out of the room, around the building three times . . .

Leader: You don't say?

Plaidman: I do.

Leader: So, now you have a real superpower?

Plaidman: Superpowers, as in more than one. For I have just had bionic inserts placed in the soles of my shoes.

Leader: Bionic inserts?

Plaidman: That's what I just said.

Leader: I'm not sure that I understand.

Plaidman: *[rolls eyes]* Sorry, I forget I'm talking to a mere mortal. What I mean is that I've had super bionic chips inserted in my shoes, so that now I can now run faster than humanly possible.

Leader: *[looks at Plaidman's shoes]* They look like regular ol' shoes to me.

Plaidman: They fool most people.

Leader: Boy, we'd love to see a demonstration, wouldn't we, boys and girls? *[allows responses]*

Plaidman: A demonstration?

Leader: That's what I just said.

Plaidman: Um . . . OK. Here goes. *[stands perfectly still for a moment]* There.

Leader: What?

Plaidman: I did it.

Leader: Did what?

Plaidman: Just a moment ago, I ran out of this room, around the building three times, appeared on a game show, won a boatload of money, went to dinner at a nice restaurant, gave the rest of the money to charity, and returned. But, with the power of my bionic shoes, to your eyes, I didn't even move.

Leader: *[looks at the kids for a long moment]* That is absolutely, positively, not possible.

SIDEKICKS

Plaidman: *[smiles]* See how well they work?

Leader: Why don't we try something simpler.

Plaidman: Put me to the test if you dare.

L: Grab the Bible.

Leader: *[looks around room, takes a Bible, and gives it to the child closest to her]* OK, see that Bible right there? It's only a few feet away. Using your *[makes quote-marks gesture]* "bionic shoes" I want you to run over, grab that Bible, and run back here. When we see you do that, we'll believe it.

Plaidman: *[concentrates on what he is about to do]* OK, no problem.

Leader: Ready . . . go!

P: *[runs in slow motion]*

Plaidman: *[makes slow-motion sounds as he runs in slow motion to the chair, takes the Bible, and runs in slow motion back and assumes same stance as he was in when he left]* Whew!

L: What was *that*?

Leader: What was *that*?

P: Proof.

Plaidman: Proof. Here I am with the Bible in my hand. Just as you asked . . . well, demanded.

Leader: It took you like 10 minutes to get the Bible!

Plaidman: That's not my fault. You're the one who said you had to see it to believe it. So, I ran in slow motion, so that you—mere mortals—could see it.

Leader: Plaidman, you are truly inexplicable.

P: I got these inserts because I needed a new direction as a superhero and to give my life greater meaning.

Plaidman: *[smiles]* Thank you. Some people might think it was silly to spend all my savings on these expensive bionic shoes. But, I needed a new direction as a superhero. It's a very competitive market, you know. So, I decided to take matters into my own hands. Now, with any luck, my life will have greater meaning.

L: What does God think?

Leader: Well, I can understand that. So, God is cool with them?

Plaidman: God?

SIDEKICKS

P: How can I know what God would want me to do?

L: Ask Him—and read your Bible!

Leader: You said that you wanted a new direction in life. You did find out what God thought you should do before you followed this direction and spent all your savings on bionic shoes, right?

Plaidman: *[long pause]* I knew I forgot something. But, how can I know what God would want me to do?

Leader: Well, you could ask Him! He's speaking to us all of the time and just wants us to listen. And, don't forget your Bible.

Plaidman: My Bible? *[pulls out his Bible and shows it to the kids proudly]* It's plaid.

Leader: I see that. The Bible has all kinds of guidance in it for our lives. In fact, look up Psalm 119:105.

P: *[reads Psalm 119:105]*

Plaidman: *[opens Bible]* Ah, here it is. Psalm 119:105. "Your word is a lamp to my feet and a light for my path." Cool! God's Word is like a flashlight!

L: God's Word always shows us the direction that we should take.

Leader: Really, it's more like a spotlight, showing us exactly the steps that we should take. God says that we're very smart if we listen to His wisdom and do what He says. His wisdom is throughout that whole book.

Plaidman: So, when I'm facing any situation, I can open my Bible and see exactly what God says I should do.

L: All of life's questions can be answered in the Bible.

Leader: Yes, sometimes you'll see a direct answer. Other times, you can see what heroes in the Bible did. But, all of life's questions can be answered in the Bible, even whether you should get bionic shoes or not.

Plaidman: *[flips through the Bible]* Ooo . . . what's that verse?

Leader: Off the top of my head, I think you want to look at James 1:22.

P: *[reads James 1:22]*

Plaidman: *[flips through Bible then reads verse]* "Do not merely listen to the word. . . . Do what it says."

L: God is more interested in us obeying His Word than taking matters into our own hands.

Leader: When it comes to doing things—for heroes or just us mere *mortals*—God is more interested in us obeying His Word than taking matters into our own hands.

P: Superpowers are overrated.

Plaidman: Ah, good point.

Leader: So, now what?

Plaidman: You mean about my bionic inserts? Well, they did come with a 30-day money-back guarantee; I guess I could return them. Maybe I don't need them so much after all. You know, being a hero with überpowers is really overrated. If you just do what God's Word says, you can defeat the bad guys. *[looks down at his plaid outfit]* This is all for the kids—they like the plaid threads.

Leader: No doubt.

Plaidman: All right then. I'm off. *[points index finger in the air]* I'm sure that somewhere out there, someone is calling for help. And, I'm ready to show them that help comes from the Lord.

Leader: Sounds like a plan.

P: *[music plays as Plaidman leaves]* Remember, God's Word makes us all heroes!

Plaidman: Remember, God's Word makes us all heroes. And, don't forget, when evil strikes, strike back—with plaid! *[music plays as Plaidman gallantly walks to the door, then pauses]* Oh, and God's Word, too. The plaid thing is cool, but you should really strike back at evil with God's Word. *[exits]*

GOD'S WORD ALWAYS SHOWS US THE DIRECTION THAT WE SHOULD TAKE.

★ CHARACTER

Walkie-Talkie Woman is a high-strung, business-type hero, ready to seek out answers to questions for anyone about anything. She is always on top of things and in control, and her perfect appearance reflects this. She prides herself on her technological abilities and is more than happy to share her findings—and technical expertise—with others.

★ PROPS

Walkie-Talkie Woman needs a lot of cell phones. Other "belt electronics" like PDAs are also good. The leader and Walkie-Talkie Woman each need to have one working cell phone so that the leader can call Walkie-Talkie Woman at the end of the skit. The leader also needs a Bible that is bookmarked at Jeremiah 29:11.

★ MUSIC

Anything that sounds like silly ring tones will work great with this skit.

★ COSTUME CREATION

Here are some thrifty suggestions for creating your own Walkie-Talkie Woman costume. Feel free to improvise! For this character, the more technology strapped to her, the better.

MICROPHONE HEADSET
so that she can always be plugged in!

PERFECT HAIR
This super-silly hero wouldn't go anywhere with less than perfect hair!

BUSINESS SUIT
Think dress for success—any power suit will do.

LONG OVERCOAT
Tuck devices into inside pockets and have some hanging from the inside lining as well.

DANGLING CORDS
Wrap old USB cords, phone charger cords, or computer connector cords around shoulders, neck, and waist. There won't be any doubt that Walkie-Talkie Woman is really connected!

CELL PHONES AND PDAs GALORE
Stuff pockets with cell phones, PDAs, MP3 players, etc. Make sure at least one phone works with a silly ring tone!

BUSINESS SHOES
No slippers here—only immaculate business shoes will do!

God Speaks to Us through His Word

God speaks to us every day—the question is, are we listening? He speaks to us personally in our hearts, and He also speaks to us through His Word. When we read His Word consistently, we find that we not only draw closer to Him, but we also are "in the know" about how He would respond to us in many situations. In this skit, Walkie-Talkie Woman makes her appearance, discovering that there are many voices vying for our attention, but there is only One that really matters.

SIDEKICKS

L: [begins lesson as usual]

Leader: All right, today's lesson is going to be a good one. First we're going to . . .
[cell phone rings loudly with a silly ring tone]

W: [stands in the back of the room; cell phone rings]
I'll get it.

Walkie: [grabs a phone off her belt] It's me. I'll get it. Feel free to continue. [answers phone]

Leader: So, as I was saying . . .

Walkie: [speaks loudly into phone] Uh-huh, yeah. No problem.

Leader: [distracted by the loud talking] Um . . . next, we're going to . . . um . . .

Walkie: [keeps talking loudly on the phone] OK. Yes. Talk to you later then. Bye-bye.

L: Are you looking for the church service for adults?

Leader: Excuse me, are you looking for the church service for adults?

W: I'm a hero.

Walkie: Me? No. Just passing through. I'm a hero, and I'm awfully busy, as usual.

Leader: You're a hero?

Walkie: Don't let the fancy business suit fool you.

Leader: We like heroes, don't we, boys and girls? [allows responses]

Walkie: [walks to the front of the room] Great! Well, I'm a special kind of hero. I'm what you call a *technological* hero.

SIDEKICKS

W: I've been enhanced by technology.

L: What's your superpower?

W: Talking on the cell phone

W: I can access the information superhighway

L: You check movie times when battling bad guys?

W: [cell phone rings]

Leader: A technological hero?

Walkie: That's right! I've been enhanced by technology! [pulls coat back to reveal cell phones, PDAs, and other gadgets]

Leader: Wow. You must have a lot of trouble with telemarketers and prank callers.

Walkie: Caller ID is my best friend.

Leader: So, what's your superpower, exactly?

Walkie: Talking on a cell phone.

Leader: Your superpower is talking on a cell phone?

Walkie: Is there an echo in here?

Leader: An echo in here? [looks around, confused]

Walkie: Yes, my power is talking on a cell phone. I know it might not seem like much, but consider this: [says with a superior tone] I have access to the information superhighway.

Leader: That sounds cool. What's there?

Walkie: Anything you want to know—news, weather, entertainment. Do you want to know the movie times at your local theater? I have them right here. [pats her coat]

Leader: Do you check movie times often when battling bad guys?

Walkie: You're mocking me, aren't you?

Leader: Mocking you?

Walkie: There's that echo again. Look, what I'm saying is that when I'm on the hunt for a bad guy, I have information at my fingertips. And, information is power.

Leader: So, what do you . . .
[phones rings with a silly ring tone]

Walkie: Oops. Excuse me. Gotta' get this. [answers phone] This is Walkie-Talkie Woman.

SIDEKICKS

	Leader:	*[mouths to kids]* Walkie-Talkie Woman?
W: *[talks on phone]*	**Walkie:**	Uh-huh. Right. You tell him I'll buy a share at four-and-a-half points and no higher. Right. Yes. Of course. And, I'll have fries with that. OK, thank you. Bye-bye, now.
	Leader:	Well, you sure can do a lot . . . *Walkie-Talkie Woman.*
W: *[shows various cell phones]*	**Walkie:**	*[pulls a phone off her belt]* And, check this out. This isn't just a phone. It's a camera, too. *[to kids, pointing phone]* Say cheese! *[pretends to take a picture; replaces the phone; pulls out another and holds it up]* This one is a music player, too. So, while I'm bustin' bad guys, I can swing to the oldies.
	Leader:	That's handy. You can keep us safe to a beat.
	Walkie:	Exactly. *[grabs another phone]* This phone records video. *[points it at a child]* Say, "Hi, mom!" Oh, isn't he a cutie-wootie! *[replaces phone]* There's virtually nothing I can't do. *[points to another phone]* This one has a GPS tracker that shows my current location so that I can get help at the press of a button.
	Leader:	It seems that you've thought of everything.
W: I can get in touch anyone, anywhere, anytime.	**Walkie:**	I owe it all to technology. I can get in touch with anyone, anywhere, anytime.
	Leader:	Anyone?
	Walkie:	Anyone.
L: How about God?	**Leader:**	There's that echo again. How about God? Can you get in touch with God?
W: I'll Google Rod's number.	**Walkie:**	Sure, what's Rod's last name? I'll Google his number. *[acts like she is "all business" and begins to pull out a phone]*
	Leader:	No, not Rod—*God.* As in, the Creator of the universe.
	Walkie:	Sure, I . . . *[looks around her, randomly touching her collection of phones]* I'm sure one of these . . . Um . . . Well, now that I think about it . . . maybe not.
L: Being in touch with God is very important.	**Leader:**	Being in touch with God is very important. In fact, it's more important than any of those fancy features on any of your phones. He's up-to-date on everything that matters.

SIDEKICKS

L: Believe it or not, I have a technology that you don't have.

L: It's the Bible.

W: [holds out hands for Bible]

W: [reads Jeremiah 29:11]
It's like God's saying that to me!

W: I have a lot of reading to do.

W: [leaves—stands just outside the door]

Walkie: I'm sure that's true. [leans in] So, do you have the inside track on some sort of technology that I don't have?

Leader: Believe it or not, I do.

Walkie: [completely shocked] No way!

Leader: I wouldn't lie to you, Walkie-Talkie Woman. You know where I live.

Walkie: I know where you work, exercise, and shop, too. So, what is this amazing technology? Give it up.

Leader: Well, sometimes God speaks to your heart, you know. But, He'll also speak to you in another way.

Walkie: Are you talking about wireless technology? Text messaging?

Leader: I'm talking about the Bible. [pulls out a Bible and shows it to Walkie-Talkie Woman]

Walkie: Look at that. It looks used.

Leader: I use it every day. The Bible is full of God's wisdom and stories about heroes who have lived for Him.

Walkie: [holds her hands out] May I?

Leader: [gives her the Bible] It's my gift to you.

Walkie: [looks through the Bible, then stops on a page] Listen to this. Here God says, " 'For I know the plans I have for you,' declares the Lord, 'plans to prosper you and not to harm you, plans to give you hope and a future.' " That's Jeremiah 29:11. Wow! It's just like God's saying that directly to me!

Leader: There's more good stuff where that came from, too.

Walkie: Well, if you'll excuse me, I have some reading to do.

Leader: No problem. We're glad that you stopped by!

Walkie: [leaves the room, reading the Bible; stops just outside the door, within earshot]

SIDEKICKS

Leader: *[turns to kids]* Shhhh! *[pulls out a cell phone and dials; from outside the room, one of Walkie-Talkie Woman's cell phone's rings]*

Walkie: *[talks loudly from outside the room]* Hello? This is Walkie-Talkie Woman.

L: *[makes prank phone call to Walkie]*

Leader: *[disguises voice]* Hello, this is *[inserts leader's last name]* Refrigeration. I'm just calling to see if your refrigerator's running.

Walkie: Huh? Well, I think so . . .

Leader: *[switches to own voice]* Then, you better go catch it! *[hangs up]*

Walkie: *[yells from outside the room]* I know that was you, *[inserts leader's name]*!

Leader: *[shrugs shoulders innocently, grinning]*

GOD IS UP-TO-DATE ON WHAT REALLY MATTERS. ARE *YOU* PLUGGED IN?

★ CHARACTER

Engorge is a bigger-than-life, hulk of a hero who has a drive and intensity matched only by professional wrestlers. He walks like a giant, talks like a giant, and if he weren't a hero, people would probably think that he was a giant.

★ PROPS

Engorge needs a small bag of potato chips, a sandwich, an apple juice box with the straw already poked in the hole (any *clear* juice is recommended), a small tomato, a cooler to hold all of the snacks with the letters "E.A.T." written on the outside, floor covering (spread on the floor before skit begins), and a small trash can. The leader needs a Bible that is bookmarked at Matthew 4:4.

★ COSTUME CREATION

Here are some thrifty suggestions for creating your own Engorge costume. Feel free to improvise! Remember, the more you can make this hero look like a professional wrestler, the better.

SANDWICH
any type—the messier, the better!

BALD HEAD
Wear a rubber "skin" cap (found at most costume stores) or tie a bandana snugly around your head.

MUSCLES (OK, STUFFING)
Stuff an oversized sweatshirt with pillows or clothing to create oversized muscles.

DEEP, BOOMING VOICE
A big booming voice for a big booming hero!

SWEATPANTS
Cut off a pair of snug fitting sweatpants at the calf to add to the big wrestler look!

SMALL COOLER
with the letters E.A.T. on the outside and all food props stored inside

TRASH CAN
Engorge is one messy hero!

FOOD
a bag of unopened chips, a small tomato, and a juice box with a straw

BARE FEET
He is way too tough to wear shoes!

LIVING POWER OF THE WORD

In today's society, people often try to gloss over the spiritual part of our lives, as though it does not exist. We talk about being physically fit, mentally fit, and socially fit, but all too often, those who are concerned about spiritual fitness are perceived as weak. In this skit, the powerful Engorge discovers that man cannot live on bread alone. God has so much more for us than we can imagine. He wants us to have a daily dose of His living Word because without spiritual wellbeing, we are entirely missing the boat.

NOTE: There is nothing like physical comedy for kids, especially when it is gross. This skit is full of gross, physical comedy. When performing, be sure to keep the lesson goal in mind. If you eat something, be sure that you clear your mouth well enough that kids can understand what you're saying, and try not get too carried away in the silliness of the moment.

SIDEKICKS

L: *[begins lesson as usual]*

Leader: Well, it's time to start our lesson today. Wow, I'm kind of hungry. Are any of you hungry? *[allows responses]*

E: *[enters]*

Engorge: *[appears at the back of room and says in a loud, booming voice]* I'm hungry!

Leader: *[startled]* Oh my! Who are you?

E: I'm a hero—where's the food?

Engorge: *[walks to the front of the room]* What do I look like? I'm a hero! My name is Engorge, member of E.A.T. Now, where's the food?

Leader: I'm sorry, we don't have any food here right now. I was just saying how hungry I was, too.

Engorge: *[stares down the leader]* You wouldn't be lying to me, now would you? Trying to keep some morsels of goodness to yourself?

Leader: Of course not. So, you said you're a member of E.A.T.?

Engorge: That's right. A proud member.

L: What is E.A.T?

Leader: What is E.A.T.?

Engorge: *[looks at the kids with a raised eyebrow]* Sounds like the word *eat* to me.

SIDEKICKS

E: You trying to make me mad?

L: What's your superpower?

L: Eating?

E: It's a super threat.

E: *[relates how he makes super threats by eating a sandwich]*

E: Aren't I super threatening?

L: I was thinking super disgusting.

Leader: So, E.A.T. doesn't stand for anything? Like "Engorge Action Team"? Anything like that?

Engorge: *[puffs up and tries to look tough]* You trying to make me mad? 'Cause I can be pretty cranky when I'm hungry!

Leader: Let's change the subject.

Engorge: Mm-hmm.

Leader: So, why don't you tell us about your superpower.

Engorge: *[relaxes and smiles]* My superpower is eating!

Leader: Your superpower is eating?

Engorge: Well, it's really more of a super threat.

Leader: I'm not sure I understand.

Engorge: It goes like this. Pretend I'm facing an enemy. Looking him right in his beady little eyes—enemies always have beady little eyes—and I say, "Stop! You'd better not rob that bank, or else!"

Leader: And he says, "Or else what?"

Engorge: And I say, "Because if you do, I'll do this!"
[pulls the sandwich out of the cooler and stuffs it into his mouth menacingly; makes a lot of noise and lets part of sandwich fall to the floor; wipes mouth with back of hand when finished]
See how effective that is? I guarantee the beady-little-eyed guy will run away. Aren't I threatening? *Super* threatening?

Leader: *[stares at Engorge in disgust]* I was thinking . . . disgusting. *Super* disgusting.

Engorge: I'll take that as a compliment.

Leader: You may want to take something for your stomach, too.

Engorge: By the way, I can do other stuff with food.

Leader: You mean other than eat it like a trash compactor?

SIDEKICKS

E: *[demonstrates his Chip Trap; makes sure that chips land on the floor covering that is already in place]*	**Engorge:** *[smiles]* Yeah, check this out. *[pulls out a bag of potato chips and squeezes it tightly, crushing the chips; opens bag and tosses the contents onto the floor]*
	Leader: What . . . what are you doing?
	Engorge: I call it the Chip Trap.
	Leader: The Chip Trap?
	Engorge: Yeah. Lay this trap in a dark hallway and if a beady-little-eyed guy comes . . . *[walks across the chips]*
	Leader: Oh! Don't do that.
	Engorge: Listen! *[walks across the chips again]*
	Leader: *[unexcited]* They're crunching.
	Engorge: Exactly! And, the beady-little-eyed guy is caught!
	Leader: Brilliant. Really. Now, who's gonna' clean that up?
	Engorge: Beady-little-eyed guy? Oh, and that doesn't even compare to my Super Soaker Mega Blaster.
	Leader: I don't want to ask. Do you want to know what his Super Soaker Mega Blaster is, boys and girls? *[allows responses]* OK, what's your Super Soaker Mega Blaster?
E: *[demonstrates his Super Soaker]*	**Engorge:** *[pulls out a juice box with a straw already in place; tilts it toward the leader]* Stand back!
	Leader: You wouldn't dare.
	Engorge: *[squeezes the box]* Super Soaker Mega Blaster!
L: How did you become a food-based hero?	**Leader:** *[jumps out of the way]* Oh—that is just . . . that's . . . oh man! Give me that. *[takes juice box and squeezes it by accident; spills more juice]* How in the world did you become a huge, food-based hero anyway?
	Engorge: Well, I had to ask myself, "Self, you want to be a hero, right? So, what can you do that no one else can do?" And, I had my answer. My self said to me, "I can eat."

SIDEKICKS

L: *[grabs the tomato and stuffs it in mouth]*

Leader: But, anyone can eat.

Engorge: *[pulls out a small tomato]* Yes, but only I can stuff an entire tomato into my mouth.

Leader: *[grabs the tomato from Engorge and stuffs the whole thing into own mouth]*

Engorge: Whoa! That's impressive! Hey, maybe you're a hero, too! I've never met a villain who can stuff a tomato all of the way into his mouth.

Leader: *[swallows]* I'm glad to be part of the club.

E: My life is all about food.

Engorge: Anyway, that's it. My life, my hero life, is all about food. Food, food, food. I love it.

L: You need more than food.

Leader: Well, that's cool. I mean, I can see how it could be a superpower. Well, I can *almost* see that anyway. But, you know, you need more than food in your life to stay alive.

Engorge: Not me.

L: *[reads Matthew 4:4]*

Leader: Everyone does. *[opens Bible]* Jesus Himself said in Matthew 4:4 that "Man does not live on bread alone."

Engorge: I agree with that. You at least need some mayonnaise.

Leader: No, what Jesus said was that we can't live on bread alone. We need to live "on every word that comes from the mouth of God."

Engorge: We need to live by God's Word?

L: The Word of God is vital to your survival.

Leader: Yes. You know that sometimes people think that in order to survive, all they need is food and water. But, that's not true. To really live, you also need to have God's Word in your heart. The words and wisdom that are in the Bible are vital to your survival.

Engorge: You know, I don't think I've ever tasted the Bible.

L: The Bible is good.

Leader: Well, let me tell you, you're missing out. It's good.

Engorge: Better than chocolate chip ice cream with chocolate syrup?

SIDEKICKS

E: My favorite food is warm sweet potatoes and honey.

Leader: What is your favorite food? What's the one food that you would do anything for, if you could have just one bite?

Engorge: *[thinks about it]* That would be sweet potatoes drenched in butter and honey. Warm.

Leader: Mmm . . . that does sound good. But get this, the Word of God is even better than that.

Engorge: Gimme, gimme, gimme! I've gotta' have it!

L: *[gives Engorge a Bible]*

Leader: *[hands over Bible]* I happen to have a Bible right here, ready for you to dig in.

E: This looks awesome!

Engorge: *[grabs the Bible, opens it, and checks out some pages]* This looks awesome! Thank you so much!

Leader: It's the least I could do.

E: *[leaves]*

Engorge: I better run! I have a lot of reading to do! *[runs out the door]*

Leader: There you go. Doesn't turning someone to God's Word make you feel good, boys and girls? *[looks down at the floor]* Hey, wait! Who's gonna' clean this up? Engorge! Come back! Aw, man!

TO REALLY LIVE, YOU NEED TO HAVE GOD'S WORD IN YOUR HEART.

★ CHARACTER

The Mysterious Mind Melder-er is about as close to being a crazy, mad scientist as one can get without actually being crazy or mad. He is convinced of his own amazing abilities and eager to share his stories and experiences—adding his own super-silly spin to them, of course.

★ PROPS

The leader needs a piece of paper containing information written in big, bold letters about the lesson and a Bible that is bookmarked at Colossians 3:13. Mind Melder-er needs a clipboard with paper attached and a pencil for jotting down any new data that he discovers.

★ COSTUME CREATION

Here are some thrifty suggestions for creating your own Mysterious Mind Melder-er costume. Feel free to improvise!

WHITE MUSTACHE
Even a superhero cannot grow one overnight, so a fake one will do—anything to add to the "mad scientist" look!

METAL HELMET
Add curled chenille craft sticks and foam balls or craft pom-poms to a metal colander.

GLASSES
Round wire-rimmed specs would look best.

WHITE LAB COAT
Ever seen a scientist without one? A short, white terry cloth robe could also be used.

METAL CHEST PROTECTOR
Use a metal cookie sheet to create this chest shield.

CLIPBOARD
to jot down any new data on mind melding

WHITE SHOES
White sneakers would work!

WHITE PANTS
to match his white lab coat and shoes

DIRECTNESS OF THE WORD

The Word of God is far more than a historical book or even a guidebook for Christians. It is literally alive, and its words can penetrate our deepest defenses, challenging and convicting even the most stubborn of us. In this skit, The Mysterious Mind Melder-er finds out that while his own soul-searching abilities are limited, God's abilities are mighty, direct, and always right on target.

SIDEKICKS

L: *[begins lesson as usual]*	**Leader:** *[holds a paper about today's lesson]* Let's get into today's message. Today, we're going to talk about . . .
M: *[enters]* Don't say a word!	**Melder-er:** *[suddenly appears at the back of the room]* Wait! Don't say another word!
	Leader: Huh? I'm sorry? Who are you?
	Melder-er: *[walks down the aisle toward the leader; both hands on his helmet like he's concentrating hard]* It's me! The Mysterious Mind Melder-er!
	Leader: *[dubiously]* Mind Melder-er?
M: I can read minds!	**Melder-er:** Right-o, my friend! I'm a hero with an amazing ability! I can read minds!
	Leader: Really?
	Melder-er: Is that so far-fetched?
	Leader: Yes?
	Melder-er: Wrong-o! It's true. I can read minds, which is how I know what you're going to teach today.
L: What am I going to teach today?	**Leader:** So, what am I going to teach?
	Melder-er: *[closes eyes; concentrates]* Don't tell me . . .
	Leader: I haven't said a word.
M: You're teaching the Bible!	**Melder-er:** You're teaching . . . the Bible!

SIDEKICKS

	Leader: Isn't that kind of obvious? We're in a church.
	Melder-er: Ah, you want me to be more specific.
	Leader: Right-o.
M: *[peeks at leader's paper with lesson title on it]*	**Melder-er:** *[concentrates]* You're teaching about . . . *[opens one eye; peeks at the piece of paper the leader is holding; says the topic]*
L: You peeked!	**Leader:** Hey, you peeked!
	Melder-er: *[pretends to write notes on his clipboard]* Nonsense! I teleported your thoughts into my head which gave me the answer!
L: I'm thinking of a number . . .	**Leader:** OK, I'm thinking of a number between 1 and one million. What is it?
	Melder-er: 431.
	Leader: No.
	Melder-er: 876.
	Leader: No.
	Melder-er: 12?
	Leader: You can't read minds, can you?
M: Did you eat cheese puffs?	**Melder-er:** I know what's wrong. Did you eat cheese puffs for breakfast?
	Leader: Cheese puffs?
	Melder-er: Yeah, you know—the squiggly orange, cheesy, crunchy puffs that taste delectably yummy?
	Leader: I know what they are. What difference does it make if I ate cheese puffs?
M: They block my mind reading.	**Melder-er:** *[rolls eyes]* Because they block my mind reading. Duh!
L: How did you become the M?	**Leader:** You know, you just haven't convinced me. How did you become The Mysterious Mind Melder-er anyway?

SIDEKICKS

M: *[tells story of girl with ball]*

Melder-er: *[puts down clipboard and begins telling his story with a lot of drama]* When I was a young man, I once saw a little girl playing with a ball. The ball rolled into the street, and suddenly, my mind-reading capabilities screamed out! I knew that she was thinking of going after it, so I went and got the ball myself. When I returned it to her, I could tell by reading her mind that she was happy.

Leader: I . . . I think you might have known that stuff without being able to read minds. What do you think, boys and girls? *[allows responses]*

Melder-er: Well, how about the time I stopped Slushman?

Leader: Do tell.

M: *[tells story of stopping Slushman]*

Melder-er: I saw the villain Slushman standing on top of a bank with 900 gallons of cherry-flavored slush. I read his mind and knew instantly that he was going to do something bad with it.

Leader: So the fact that a villain had 900 gallons of slush on top of a bank wasn't clue enough?

Melder-er: This is my story.

Leader: Sorry.

M: I went to the store and bought an industrial heater.

Melder-er: So, I rushed to the store across the street and bought an industrial heater. When I came out, Slushman had already frozen the bank in a mountain of cherry slush. He was bolting out the front door holding big cloth bags in each hand. *[pauses and taps metal helmet]* I read his mind and knew that he was stealing money from the bank.

Leader: You think?

Melder-er: It's a good thing I do think, bub, for I quickly turned on the heater and melted the bank and the Slushman. I saved the day!

Leader: Wow, that was quite heroic . . . but again, not sure if I'm convinced that you can read anyone's mind. I think anyone would have known the stuff you've told us about.

SIDEKICKS

	Melder-er: Would they?
L: Only one thing can read our thoughts, secrets and feelings.	**Leader:** As far as I know, there's only one thing that can truly read us—not just our thoughts, but also our innermost secrets and feelings.
	Melder-er: *[holds up clipboard and pencil, ready to write down what the leader says]* What's that?
L: The Bible.	**Leader:** *[holds up a Bible]* The Bible—God's Word.
	Melder-er: It can read our thoughts, secrets, and feelings?
	Leader: Without a doubt.
	Melder-er: How? It's a book.
L: Say someone does something bad to you.	**Leader:** Oh, this is much more than a book. Let's say someone does something bad to you.
	Melder-er: Like make fun of the metal hat on your head.
	Leader: Yeah, let's say he says that your hat looks like a salad bowl.
	Melder-er: *[nods in understanding]* Mmm-hmmm.
	Leader: You tell him it's OK. It doesn't bother you that he said that. But, deep down inside, his comment really bugs you.
M: *[remembers what the Gooberator did to him]*	**Melder-er:** Oh! Like the time I battled the Gooberator and he spread his sticky, slippery, sludgy goo all over my feet. I fell over like a lead balloon.
	Leader: *[pauses; looks horrified]* OK, yes, that might be something hard to forgive.
M: Now I wear my super-durable hat and chest protector.	**Melder-er:** Well, I wasn't so concerned about that. But, he dented my metal hat. Was not cool. So now, of course, I wear my super durable metal hat *and* chest protector. *[pats metal chest protector]*
L: *[reads Colossians 3:13]*	**Leader:** Ahh, I understand. Well, let's say one day you're reading the Word, and you read Colossians 3:13, *[opens Bible and reads]* "Forgive as the Lord forgave you."

SIDEKICKS

Melder-er: Whoa, that's good.

Leader: *[nods in agreement]* And, while reading it, you suddenly remember that day with the Gooberator, and you realize that the Bible just read your mail. God's telling you to forgive the Gooberator because, after all, God has forgiven you of far worse.

Melder-er: W-O-W. Wow. The Bible can read that kind of stuff in us?

Leader: And so much more. *[hands Bible to Mind Melder-er]*

Melder-er: *[takes Bible and removes metal hat]* You know, I think the Bible might work better than this thing.

Leader: I can guarantee it.

M: I need to start reading.

Melder-er: Well, if you'll excuse me then, *[acts distracted as he opens Bible, flips pages, and heads toward the door]* I need to start reading. God has my number.

L: Even cheese puffs can't stop Him.

Leader: And, even cheese puffs can't stop Him. So, go ahead and chow down while you study.

Melder-er: *[stops and turns to leader]* Ah, you read my mind.

GOD'S WORD CAN READ OUR INNERMOST THOUGHTS.

★ CHARACTER

Chick Chameleon is an extremely optimistic, outrageously colorful, bubbly girl who just wants to be able to sneak up on villains, but she can't seem to find a way to be herself in the process!

★ PROPS

The leader needs a Bible that is bookmarked at 1 Peter 1:16, John 17:16, and Romans 12:2.

★ COSTUME CREATION

Here are some thrifty suggestions for creating your own Chick Chameleon costume. Feel free to improvise! For this character's costume, use as many contrasting patterns and colors as you can.

COLORFUL CLOWN WIG
Wear an outrageously colorful wig or color hair with washable hair paints.

BRIGHT, COLORFUL MAKEUP
Have fun painting your face with shapes and patterns!

WILDLY COLORFUL SHIRT
We all have one hidden in our closets, don't we? If not, visit a thrift store.

BIG SMILE
Remember, this hero is extremely optimistic!

BELT
This could be made from a rope, scarf, or colorful material.

OUTRAGEOUSLY COLORFUL CAPE
Use fabric, a sheet, or a skirt that has been cut in half.

WILDLY COLORFUL FRUMPY PANTS
with bright bold patterns that contrast with the shirt

COLORFUL MISMATCHED SOCKS
Getting the picture?

NO SHOES
easier to sneak up on villainous villains!

THE WORD SETS YOU APART

People generally like to fit in, not to be labeled as "different," and to be a part of the crowd. Even those of us who try to be distinctly different often have a tight social group in which being different is the norm. God says that living outside the societal norm is not only OK, it is also required if we are living for Him. In this skit, Chick Chameleon learns that when she lives for Jesus, she is not able to blend in with the crowd, and that is OK. In fact, there is nothing as exciting as living according to the Word.

SIDEKICKS

L: *[begins lesson as usual; distracted by Chameleon entrance]*

C: *[slides in quietly along a wall]*

C: Ignore me!

C: You can see me?

Leader:	Today's message is all about living for . . . er . . . uh . . . *[looks toward back of room]* *[Chick Chameleon sneaks in and slides along a wall, as though painting the wall with her back; freezes in a comical stance, her arms and legs bent in unique combinations; leader stares at her comically waiting for all the kids to notice her as well]* Um . . . excuse me. Are you looking for the circus?
Chameleon:	*[without moving her lips]* Shhhhh!
Leader:	Huh?
Chameleon:	*[without moving her lips]* Just ignore me! Pretend I'm not here!
Leader:	*[to kids]* OK . . . well, as I was saying, today's message is about . . . *[distracted; addresses Chick Chameleon]* I'm sorry. It's kind of hard to just ignore you. Is there anything we can do to help?
Chameleon:	Oh, man! *[pulls off the wall]* You can see me? I can't *believe* you can see me!
Leader:	Actually, I think we can *all* see you. Can you all see her, boys and girls? *[allows responses]*
Chameleon:	You're kidding me! Is there a hidden camera or something? Oh, man! You weren't supposed to be able to see me!

SIDEKICKS

C: I'm supposed to blend in perfectly with my surroundings.

C: This is so frustrating! Bad guys can see me, too.

L: Could it be your colorful outfit?

Leader: I'm sorry, but you really stick out like a sore thumb. Are you supposed to be invisible?

Chameleon: Almost. I'm supposed to blend in perfectly with my surroundings. For, I am a hero! I am *[throws herself against the wall again]* Chick Chameleon! *[freezes in a pose]*

Leader: We can still see you.

Chameleon: *[without moving her lips]* You can *all* see me?

Leader: *[to children]* Can you all see her? *[allows responses]*

Chameleon: *[pulls off wall]* Man!

Leader: Sorry, it's just . . . actually, it's hard *not* to see you.

Chameleon: This is so frustrating! Do you know how frustrating this is?

Leader: You're a hero, but your superpower isn't working? I imagine that *is* frustrating.

Chameleon: *[walks to front of room beside leader]* You have *no* idea. I'm supposed to be a hero—sneak up on bad guys and stop them in their tracks. But, they can all *see* me! I must be doing something wrong.

Leader: You don't think that it could have anything to do with your colorful outfit?

Chameleon: Why do you say that?

Leader: It's a bit . . . loud. I could hear it from across the room.

Chameleon: *[fluffs her hair; smooths her outfit]* A girl has to be fashionable. Especially when she's a hero. I'm in the public eye a lot, you know.

Leader: Maybe it's just the surroundings you choose. You know, stand in front of an exploding rainbow and I bet we'd hardly see you.

Chameleon: OK, let me try again.

C: *[tries a few more ways of blending in]*

L: Bending?

C: *[jumps up into the audience and tries to blend in]*

L: Not blending in may not be a bad thing.

C: The Super-Silly Hero Justice League will revoke my license.

L: Standing out may not be a bad thing.

C: Have you ever been expected to just blend in?

Leader: Actually, I was just kidd . . .

Chameleon: *[suddenly drops to the floor like a sack of potatoes with arms and legs bent in different directions]*

Leader: What are you doing?

Chameleon: *[without moving her lips]* Blending.

Leader: Bending?

Chameleon: *[moving her lips]* Blending! BLuh! BLuh! Blend! Blending!

Leader: I don't think it's working.

Chameleon: *[leaps up and jumps into the audience, sits among the children and dramatically tries to blend in; imitates nearby children; grabs objects like a child's Bible, hat, jacket, etc., to use to blend in; says without moving her lips]* Ha! You can't see me now!

Leader: Can you see her, boys and girls? *[allows responses]*

Chameleon: Man! *[returns to the front of the room]* I gotta' tell you, this hero stuff isn't as easy as it looks.

Leader: Actually, that may not be such a bad thing.

Chameleon: Are you kidding? What am I supposed to do? The Super-Silly Hero Justice League will revoke my license!

Leader: There's a Super-Silly Hero Justice League?

Chameleon: *[caught off guard, talks fast]* You didn't hear it from me. I didn't say anything.

Leader: Look, I really don't think standing out is *that* bad.

Chameleon: Have you ever been a hero with superpowers?

Leader: Well, no.

Chameleon: Have you ever been expected to just blend in with the crowd?

SIDEKICKS

L: God doesn't want us to blend in.
[reads 1 Peter 1:16]

L: God gave us the Bible so that we could live by what it says even if that sets us apart.

L: *[paraphrases John 17:16 and Romans 12:2 NLT]*

L: Not blending in means that you might be doing something right.

Leader: Actually, yes.

Chameleon: Really?

Leader: Sure. I think that we all feel pressure to blend in with the crowd sometimes. But, that's why I don't think this is bad news for you.

Chameleon: Why not?

Leader: Because, God doesn't want us to blend in with the crowd. Here, let me show you. *[grabs a Bible]* Here, in 1 Peter 1:16, God says, "Be holy, because I am holy." Living holy means living differently from the crowd, doesn't it?

Chameleon: Yes. God said that?

Leader: He sure did. That's one reason He gave us His Word, the Bible. He wants us to live by what it says instead of what anyone else says. That may set us apart, but that's OK. That's the way it should be.

Chameleon: That's cool! But, can't I live for God and blend in at the same time? That sure would make things easier for me.

Leader: I suppose that's true, but God never said living for Him would be easy. In fact, *[looks in the Bible]* He said in John 17:16 that we may *live* in this world, but we're not *of* it. And, in Romans 12:2, God says that we aren't supposed to copy the behavior of the world. Learning about God and His Word changes our minds and hearts and makes us different.

Chameleon: Whew! I gotta' tell you, that sure is a load off my mind. Ever since I discovered I couldn't blend in, I thought I was doomed.

Leader: On the contrary, it may mean that you're doing something right. *And,* it means you might finally be able to get rid of that ridiculous costume.

Chameleon: What ridiculous costume?

Leader: *[talks fast; tries to cover]* Nothing. I didn't say anything. You didn't hear it from me.

Chameleon: Very well then. I guess I'd better go find a new way to be a hero since there's no way that I can—or would want to—blend in anymore.

L: I'm glad we're seeing your true colors.

Leader: I'm glad we're finally seeing your true colors.

C: *[runs into wall]*

Chameleon: Me, too! Good-bye then, all! Nice to see you . . . and have you see me!

[waves as she walks to back of room; misses door and comically runs into the wall beside it]

Ouch! Whoops! Hey, I didn't see it there!

L: See how painful blending in can be?

Leader: See how painful blending in can be?

Chameleon: *[rubs her nose]* No kidding! *[exits]*

**DON'T BLEND IN!
BE SET APART BY GOD'S WORD!**

★ CHARACTER

Infomercial Guy is a slick-looking salesman. Everything about him screams, "Have I got a deal for you!" Any passerby would think that he has all the answers to achieving success in life, despite the fact that he's still searching for the ultimate, and final, truth.

★ PROPS

Infomercial Guy needs a thick book with a fake cover that reads *Collection of Guphygai Wisdom* (pronounced *goo-FAY-guy*) and a briefcase to hold the book. The leader needs a Bible that is bookmarked at Matthew 7:15, Colossians 2:8, and Matthew 10:8.

★ COSTUME CREATION

Here are some thrifty suggestions for creating your own Infomercial Guy costume. Feel free to improvise! For this character, just think "Sunday best."

PERFECT HAIR
Gotta' look good for the cameras!

GLASSES
They make him look smart!

WIDE SMILE
big, toothy, fake smile that says, "Trust me!"

IRONED SHIRT AND TIE
everything must scream success!

SUIT JACKET
He's an executive salesman, after all.

THICK BOOK
thick book with a fake cover that reads, *Collection of Guphygai Wisdom*

BRIEFCASE
to hold *Collection of Guphygai Wisdom* book

IRONED SLACKS
to go along with his impeccable suit jacket

SHINY SHOES
the shinier, the better!

COLLECTION OF GUPHYGAI WISDOM

TIMELESSNESS OF GOD'S WORD

There are a lot of teachings in the world today that conflict with the truth of God's Word. Colossians 2:8 NLT reads, "Don't let anyone lead you astray with empty philosophy and high-sounding nonsense that come from human thinking and from the evil powers of this world, and not from Christ." In this skit, kids will meet Infomercial Guy, who quickly learns that the collection of teachings he's been peddling do not hold a candle to the true and living Word of God—a timeless truth that holds its own against any humanistic definition of truth.

SIDEKICKS

L: *[begins lesson as usual]*

I: *[enters]*

I: Let me have a moment.

I: *[introduces himself]*

I: My specialty is the power of persuasion!

Leader:	All right, kids, today's topic is something special.
Info:	*[appears at the back of the room, smiling widely and looking confident; speaks in a loud salesman's voice]* Did you say that you're looking for something special?
Leader:	Oh—yes, I did. We're getting ready for today's lesson.
Infomercial:	*[walks to the front of the room]* Well, before you get started, why not let me have just a moment. I guarantee you that it'll be well worth your time.
Leader:	And, you are . . . ?
Infomercial:	I am Infomercial Guy, a hero of tomorrow, with a message for today—as seen on TV.
Leader:	I don't think I've ever seen you on TV.
Infomercial:	I'm on mostly cable channels at 3 A.M. I get the security guard crowd.
Leader:	I see. Why do they call you Infomercial Guy?
Infomercial:	My specialty is the power of persuasion! I can convince *anyone* of *anything* in 30 minutes or less.
Leader:	Wow, that's quite a superpower. How did you learn to do that?

SIDEKICKS

I: This is the *Collection of Guphygai Wisdom.*

Infomercial: I'm glad you asked! *[puts down briefcase and opens it; pulls out a thick book]* This, my friend, is the *Collection of Guphygai [pronounced goo-FAY-guy] Wisdom!*

Leader: The *Collection of Guphygai Wisdom?*

Infomercial: *[says as if performing infomercial]* Yes, with it, you—like me—can become a Guphygai warrior! You'll find life more rewarding than ever as you learn about the ancient teachings of the Guphygai people. You'll learn all of their secrets to life, including how to be truly happy living in a mud hut *and* be wow'ed by their thought-provoking philosophy of seashells. As a special bonus, you'll learn a little origami, too. *[flashes big smile as if on TV]*

L: Looks like the Collection of *Goofy Guy* Wisdom.

Leader: *[reads title on book]* You sure that's pronounced goo-FAY-guy? It looks like GOOF-ee-guy. The Collection of Goofy Guy Wisdom.

I: It's ancient wisdom.

Infomercial: Make fun if you want, but I'll be the one laughing to the bank. This is a book of ancient wisdom from the Guphygai warriors and their experiences serving their warrior god, Guphygai. It's full of fascinating information. See how thick it is? *[flips through the pages]*

Leader: Serving Goofy Guy?

Infomercial: Goo-FAY-guy. They learned that there was great power in serving Guphygai with his great wisdom and his Mercedes Benz.

Leader: Uh-huh.

Infomercial: But, wait! There's more! *[says as if he's on an infomercial]* Legend has it, Guphygai was a very smart and talented god—*in fact,* he could make any origami bird in ten seconds flat! That's not an easy feat, mind you.

L: There's only one true God.

Leader: No, I guess it isn't. But, this is "god" as in, "small g." In other words, a *pretend* god. Because there's only one *true* God.

Infomercial: Pretend? I don't think so! I've seen his origami birds, they are very lifelike. And besides, *someone* had to come up with this great wisdom. What? You think it came out of thin air?

Super-Silly Hero Skits • CD-204058

SIDEKICKS

I: It is smart not to be a criminal, but it is a crime not to be smart.

I: This book contains great predictions about the end of the world.

I: According to the book, the world will end in 2002!

I: How much would you pay?

L: We're not interested.

Leader: Do you really want me to answer that?

Infomercial: Just listen to an example of his wisdom. *[opens the book and reads]* "It is smart not to be a criminal, but it is a crime not to be smart." *[dramatically pauses and thinks about it]* Wow, huh? That is so deep, I'm not even sure what it means.

Leader: I'm not sure *any* of us know what it means!

Infomercial: This book contains not only the *wisdom* of Guphygai, but also his *great prediction* about the end of the world!

Leader: *[unimpressed]* Really?

Infomercial: Yes, according to this book, there will be a great battle and the world will end in 2002!

Leader: 2002? Um . . . that was years ago. The world hasn't ended.

Infomercial: *[nods very seriously]* Makes you think, doesn't it?

Leader: *[nods]* You could say that.

Infomercial: How much would you pay for a volume of wisdom like this? $200? $300? More? You can have it today for only three easy payments of $19.95! All major credit cards accepted. *[flashes another big smile as he holds up the book]*

Leader: That's $60!

Infomercial: Actually, it's $59.85. A bargain basement price! And, if you order now, I'll emboss your name on the cover—up to six characters—in gold! Act now and you'll also get . . .

Leader: Infomercial Guy, we are not interested.

Infomercial: I'm sorry?

Leader: We don't need Goofy Guy's book, do we, boys and girls? *[allows responses]*

SIDEKICKS

Infomercial: Wait! This deal will only be available for the next 48 hours! The first five callers will also get a complete set of those cute little corn on the cob holders—you know, that you stick in each end of the cob so that you don't burn your fingers? They just make me giggle. Don't they make you gig . . .

L: We have something better—the Bible.

Leader: Sorry, we have something better.

Infomercial: Better than Goofy Guy's—er, Guphygai's—wisdom?

Leader: We have [pulls out Bible] the Bible. The Word of God.

Infomercial: [looks mildly interested] I haven't seen that one.

Leader: Then, you're really missing out. This book was written by the true God, not some "legend" who makes origami birds.

Infomercial: You mean *the* God of the universe?

Leader: Is there another?

Infomercial: [genuinely] Wow. Color me impressed.

L: [reads Matthew 7:15 and paraphrases Colossians 2:8 NLT]

Leader: The wisdom inside this book makes *sense.* Such as, [opens Bible] "Watch out for false prophets." That's Matthew 7:15. It also says not to let anyone fool you with empty philosophies which depend on human thinking rather than the Word of God. That's in Colossians 2:8.

Infomercial: [puts the Guphygai book aside] That *is* good.

L: God has a plan for you—and it didn't end in 2002.

Leader: This book also talks about how the Lord is coming back soon! He has a plan for you—and it didn't end back in 2002. His plans for you are happening now!

Infomercial: Wow! Can I get more if I act now?

Leader: This is *all* that you need. [points to Bible] But, you do need to leave Goofy Guy behind.

Infomercial: I can do that. How much will this cost? Do you have an easy payment plan?

SIDEKICKS

L: *[refers to Matthew 10:8]*

Leader: All it costs is your heart, my friend. This wisdom is free. God says we have received His Word freely, and we should freely give it. That's Matthew 10:8.

I: *[throws his Guphygai book aside]*

Infomercial: Whoa! *[takes Bible]* I'll take it! I'm done being a Goofy Guy warrior. I'm ready to become a warrior for God. I'm off to read! *[tosses the Guphygai book into a trash can and then heads to the door; stops and turns around]* Um . . . wait, what about the Guphygai people?

Leader: God loves them and His wisdom is free for them, as well!

Infomercial: *[looks relieved and continues walking]* Ok, then. You've convinced me!

Leader: How about that? In 30 minutes or less.

I: *[leaves]*

Infomercial: *[stops in his tracks]* Hey, that was my line.

Leader: What can I say? The Word stands on its own. See you soon, Infomercial Guy!

ACT NOW TO GET THE FREE, TRUE WISDOM OF GOD'S WORD.

★ CHARACTER

Infomercial Guy is back! He is a slick-looking salesman who is always trying to make a buck and really believes in his product! Any passerby would think that he has all of the answers to achieving success in life, despite the fact that he is still searching for the ultimate, and final, truth.

★ PROPS

Infomercial Guy needs a thick, oversized book with a cover that reads, *New and Improved Bible.* For easy reference, copy the passages that are to be read from this book and place them inside the book. Infomercial Guy also needs a briefcase to carry the book.

★ COSTUME CREATION

Here are some thrifty suggestions for creating your own Infomercial Guy costume. Feel free to improvise! For this character, just think "Sunday best."

PERFECT HAIR
Gotta' look good for
the cameras!

GLASSES
They make him look smart!

OVERCONFIDENT SMILE
always ready to
make a sale!

THICK BOOK
with a fake cover that
reads, *New and
Improved Bible*

SUIT JACKET
He's an executive
salesman, after all.

**IRONED SHIRT
AND TIE**
everything must
scream success!

BRIEFCASE
to hold his
latest product

IRONED SLACKS
to go along with his
impeccable suit jacket

SHINY SHOES
the shinier
the better!

FINAL AUTHORITY OF THE WORD

The Word of God is the final authority on everything—it is absolute truth. Often, people look for ways to stretch or change the truth to fit into their personal definitions of God. But, God does not need our help in defining who He is. In this skit, Infomercial Guy returns, new and improved . . . or maybe not. He finds out that changing God's Word to fit our own beliefs is not a good idea. Instead, God's Word should *form* our beliefs.

NOTE: Most skits in this book can stand alone, but the presentation of this skit needs to occur sometime after the Infomercial Guy, Guphygai Warrior skit to be fully enjoyed.

SIDEKICKS

L: *[begins lesson as usual]*

I: *[enters]*

Leader: I'm so glad each of you could be here today because we have something extra special in store . . .

Infomercial: *[appears at the back of the room with briefcase in hand; speaks in an over-the-top TV salesman voice]*

Did someone say "extra special"? If so, you must be calling me! The new and improved Infomercial Guy!

Leader: Hey, it's Infomercial Guy. Wow, last time we saw you, you found out that your Goofy Guy book wasn't any good—it couldn't stand up to the power of the Bible.

Infomercial: *[walks to the front of the room, swinging his briefcase]* That's right! I have learned *so much* from the Bible, and I have you guys to thank for it. As I said, I'm a new and improved hero! Fighting evil better than ever!

L: *[notices the briefcase]*
Are you still selling Goofy Guy books?

Leader: *[looks at the briefcase]* What's that? Are you still selling those Goofy Guy books?

Infomercial: Are you kidding? Once I discovered that the Bible was so much better, I dumped the Goofy Guy book like a hot potato! I bet you can't wait to see what I have in this briefcase.

Leader: I don't know. Do you want to see what he has, boys and girls? *[allows responses]*

SIDEKICKS

I: Here's the Bible—new and improved!

I: Everything can be made better.

L: God wrote the Bible the way He wanted it.

I: *[reads updated manger scene]*

Infomercial: I knew you would. Check this out! *[opens briefcase and pulls out a thick book]* Here it is—the Bible, new and improved by me! Infomercial Guy!

Leader: A new and improved Bible?

Infomercial: Yessiree! I know what you're thinking—the Bible was nearly perfect, right?

Leader: Actually, I was thinking that it is *entirely* perfect.

Infomercial: Everything has room for improvement! If I met the Easter Bunny, I'd say, "Hey, why not try out a pogo stick?" If I met Santa Claus, I'd say, "Why not move your workshop to the Bahamas?" Everything can be made better if you put your mind to it.

Leader: But, God is real, and He wrote the Bible exactly the way He wanted it.

Infomercial: Think so? Check this out. First, I updated it for modern living. For instance, what happened when Jesus was born?

Leader: What? You mean the part where He was put in a manger because there was no room for them in the inn?

Infomercial: Yeah, so I updated it. *[reads from book]* "Lo and behold, Jesus was born in the bedding section of a department store, for there was no room for them at a four-star hotel." See, doesn't that just make it come alive?

Leader: Born in . . . what? . . . but that's messing with history.

Infomercial: No, it's *updating* history because we live differently now. I haven't really changed any of the meaning.

Leader: *[looks at boys and girls dubiously]*

Infomercial: I can tell you're not sold. *[says like an infomercial line]* But, wait! There's more! Let me give you another example.

Leader: We can't wait.

Infomercial: Do you know the verse James 2:26?

Leader: Let's see. Isn't that the one that says, "Faith without deeds is dead?"

I: *[reads updated James 2:26]*

Infomercial: Right—only I improved it. *[reads from book]* Now, it says, "Faith without deeds is a little bit sleepy."

Leader: *[totally shocked]* A little bit sleepy?

Infomercial: Well, you know, *dead* is such a strong word. We don't want to run the risk of offending anyone. So, we'll just say, *[speaks in a soft, soothing voice]* "Faith without deeds is a little bit sleepy." Isn't that nice? We're giving faith a little bit of yawn time. *[yawns]*

Leader: Speaking of yawning . . .

I: *[reads updated Hebrews 11:6]*

Infomercial: Or, how about this one . . . *[reads from book]* "Without a mustache, it is impossible to please God." Hebrews 11:6.

L: *[correctly quotes Hebrews 11:6]*

Leader: What? That verse is supposed to say, "Without *faith* it is impossible to please God." Why did you change it?

Infomercial: Simplicity. A lot of people don't know what faith is. But everyone knows what a mustache is. *That* is something everyone can do—grow a mustache.

Leader: Girls can't grow mustaches!

Infomercial: Actually, I may have to disagree . . .

Leader: *[gets frustrated; holds up hand to stop]* Enough! Enough!

Infomercial: Wait! Don't you want to hear about Jesus coming back to Earth riding a T-Rex? That's in the new and improved Revelation!

L: You can't do this! The Word is the way God wants it.

Leader: *Infomercial Guy!* You can't change the Bible to say whatever you want it to say! The Word says that the Lord is the same yesterday, today, and forever. He doesn't change—Hebrews 13:8—the *real* version. He gave us His Word exactly the way He wanted it. He doesn't want us to change it. In fact, He says that anyone who changes His Word is in *big* trouble!

SIDEKICKS

I: In my version of the Bible, it says He would prefer you consult a lawyer.

L: Only the real Word is the truth.

I: *[admits his error]* I thought I could make some money.

L: The Bible is the final authority.

L: *[drops "improved" book on the ground; suggests paperweights]*

Infomercial: Actually, in my version of the Bible, it just says He would prefer that you consult a lawyer before changing anything.

Leader: But here's the thing: *Your* version of the Bible *doesn't matter.* It's not the truth. Only God's version of the Bible matters. *It* is the final authority. And, if you change it, you'll have to answer to God.

Infomercial: Oh. *[looks a little worried]* That doesn't sound like fun. Could I just send Him a sticky note?

Leader: Do you really want to try that?

Infomercial: You're right. I should have an assistant do it.

Leader: What do you think, boys and girls? Should he change the Bible to say whatever he wants it to say? *[allows responses]*

Infomercial: Well, perhaps you're right. Maybe this wasn't the *best* idea I've ever had. It's just that I thought I could make a lot of money on this one—you know, three easy payments of $19.95 and all.

Leader: But God's Word isn't for sale, my friend. Never has been.

Infomercial: So, I guess I need to stay with the one you use, huh?

Leader: Yep, it's the absolute truth, the final authority. You can judge good and bad ideas by what it says in here. And, it says that making your own version of the Bible is a very bad idea.

Infomercial: Wow. So, what do you think I should do with the 600 crates of these that I just had delivered from the printer?

Leader: *[takes "improved" book and drops it on the ground with a thud]* Have you thought about going into the business of selling paperweights?

Infomercial: *[nods and grins]* Or, it could make a nice doorstop.

Leader: *[smiles]* Now, that's something that I think God would approve of!

L: Your ideas are getting better and better.

I: Gotta' go. I have lots of ideas to write down!

Infomercial: Or, fireplace kindling! Or, we could shred them and make kitty litter!

Leader: Your ideas are getting better by the minute.

Infomercial: *[picks up the book]* I better go, my friend. Gotta' write down these ideas before I lose them! *[walks quickly out of room]*

Leader: Bye, Infomercial Guy! Sounds like you're becoming a new and improved hero every day.

THE BIBLE IS THE FINAL AUTHORITY.

The Inexplicable Plaidman, page 7

The Squeak, page 25

Jamma Jamma, page 13

Rewind Girl, page 31

Polka Dot, page 19

Plaidman: Bionic Edition, page 37

Super-Silly Hero Skits • CD-204058

Chick Chameleon, page 61

Walkie-Talkie Woman, page 43

Infomercial Guy, Guphygai Warrior, page 67

Engorge, Member of E.A.T., page 49

The Mind Melder-er, page 55

The New and Improved Infomercial Guy, page 73